Sport Sponsorship Ins

Sponsorship is a vital area of contemporary sport business. This book offers a concise and practice-focused introduction to sport sponsorship, including an explanation of key concepts, a survey of the key tools required to be a successful practitioner, and insights into real-world practice from authors with extensive industry and academic experience.

Covering sport at all levels, from professional to grassroots, and including international cases and examples throughout, the book demonstrates that sport sponsorship works if done correctly. Drawing on the latest cutting-edge research, it introduces the core principles of sport sponsorship and shows how to get maximum value at each stage of the sponsorship process, from plan to activation, servicing and evaluation, for sponsor, property or agency.

Requiring no prior knowledge of sport sponsorship, and full of real-world examples of best practice, this is the perfect primer for any student or industry professional looking to improve and deepen their understanding of this core element of modern sport business.

Norm O'Reilly is Dean of the Graduate School of Business at the University of Maine. Recognized as a leading scholar in the business of sports, he is widely published and is highly engaged in the sponsorship industry globally as Partner Consultant with the T1 Agency. He is the lead researcher on the Canadian Sponsorship Landscape Study, now in its fifteenth edition. Dr. O'Reilly is a Fellow of the North American Society for Sport Management and was awarded the Career Achievement Award by the American Marketing Association's Sport Marketing Special Interest Group.

Gashaw Abeza is Professor in the Department of Kinesiology at Towson University, USA and currently provides consultancy services to a range of sport organizations around the world. He also serves on the editorial boards of eight different academic journals: *International Journal of Sport Communication*; *Sport, Business, and Management*; *Journal of Relationship Marketing*; *International Journal of eSports Research*; *Journal of Global Sport Management*, *Sport Marketing Quarterly*; *International Journal of Sports Marketing and Sponsorship*; and the newly launched *Sport Management Digest*.

Mark Harrison is Founder of the T1 Agency in Toronto, Canada, and a leading figure in the sponsorship and marketing industries. He also created the global sponsorship conference, SponsorshipX. Mark also inspired and launched several new initiatives in 2020, collectively referred to as The MH3 Group, a group of ventures spanning from advertising and sponsorship marketing to integrated communications and education.

Sport Business Insights
Series Editors
Aaron C.T. Smith, Loughborough University, UK
Constantino Stavros, RMIT University, Australia

Sport Business Insights is a series that aims to cut through the clutter, providing concise and relevant introductions to an array of contemporary topics related to the business of sport. Readers – including passionate practitioners, curious consumers and sport students alike - will discover direct and succinct volumes, carefully curated to present a useful blend of practice and theory. In a highly readable format, and prepared by leading experts, this series shines a spotlight on subjects of currency in sport business, offering a systematic guide to critical concepts and their practical application.

Available in this series:

Sport Branding Insights
Constantino Stavros and Aaron C.T. Smith

Sport Sponsorship Insights
Norm O'Reilly, Gashaw Abeza and Mark Harrison

For more information about this series, please visit: https://www.routledge.com

Sport Sponsorship Insights

**Norm O'Reilly,
Gashaw Abeza and
Mark Harrison**

Routledge
Taylor & Francis Group

LONDON AND NEW YORK

First published 2022
by Routledge
2 Park Square, Milton Park, Abingdon, Oxon OX14 4RN

and by Routledge
605 Third Avenue, New York, NY 10158

Routledge is an imprint of the Taylor & Francis Group, an informa business

British Library Cataloguing-in-Publication Data
A catalogue record for this book is available from the British Library

Library of Congress Cataloging-in-Publication Data
Names: O'Reilly, Norm, 1973– author. | Abeza, Gashaw,
author. | Harrison, Mark (T1 Agency founder) author.
Title: Sport sponsorship insights / Norm O'Reilly,
Gashaw Abeza and Mark Harrison.
Description: Abingdon, Oxon ; New York, NY : Routledge, 2022. |
Series: Sport business insights | Includes bibliographical
references and index.
Identifiers: LCCN 2021025461 | ISBN 9780367723941
(hardback) | ISBN 9780367723958 (paperback) |
ISBN 9781003154631 (ebook)
Subjects: LCSH: Sports sponsorship.
Classification: LCC GV716 .O74 2022 | DDC 796.06/9—dc23
LC record available at https://lccn.loc.gov/2021025461

ISBN: 978-0-367-72394-1 (hbk)
ISBN: 978-0-367-72395-8 (pbk)
ISBN: 978-1-003-15463-1 (ebk)

DOI: 10.4324/9781003154631

Typeset in Times New Roman
by codeMantra

Contents

Preface

This book is about sponsorship, an important source of revenue for sport organizations, venues and athletes, as well as a valuable promotional tool for brands. Relatively new to the marketing literature, sponsorship has thrived since the turn of the Millennium and is currently facing the same reality that many areas of marketing are encountering. That reality is characterized by the global movements around digitization, social justice, and the COVID-19 global pandemic.

We wrote this book with the objective to provide those who are new to (or who want to enter) the sport sponsorship industry with three specific objectives in mind as to what we wanted our readers to take away.

First, given the rapid rate of change in the business world, sport sponsorship professionals need a clear understanding of their industry and the concept of sponsorship. By "clear understanding", we mean by the knowledge of the current state of sponsorship, its tactics, and its frameworks, including a baseline understanding of the field's history and conceptual roots, and background about the needs of its stakeholders.

Second, and perhaps most importantly, there are a set of tools that are essential for any sponsorship professional – brand, property, or agency side – where a "savoir faire" (i.e., know-how) of each of these tools is essential to success in sponsorship. These tools include four primary ones, namely valuation, evaluation, activation, and servicing. Importantly, this is not a high level tool-kit or "sponsorship for dummies" book. For each of these tools, we will share established processes, build them out, and provide clear directions for their use.

Finally, and this is sprinkled throughout the book, we wanted to share our global experiences with you. Our insights. Our travels. Our successes. Our projects. Our mistakes. Although we all hold Canadian citizenship, we have lived, worked, traveled, spectated, volunteered, spoken, consulted, organized, and participated in sport – from professional to grassroots – in more than 50 countries, on all corners of the globe. These broad range of experiences include Olympic Games, Super Bowls, FIFA World Cups, Paralympic Games, Continental Championships, National Championships, NCAA Bowl Games, Arctic Games, Youth Games and Indigenous Games, and triathlons and road races.

And, as a reader, you may ask "what will the achievement of these three objectives allow me to do?" Well, it is our collective hope that you will put down this book and be able to (i) clearly outline how, why, and when sponsorship works, (ii) apply (and share with your colleagues) a set of tools for any sponsorship in which you will be involved, and (iii) not only apply but also improve the outcomes for every entity involved – sponsors, properties, and agencies.

Thank you. Enjoy the read.

Norm O'Reilly, Gashaw Abeza, and Mark Harrison
Summer 2021

Acknowledgments

The authors would like to sincerely thank Michael Alcorn for his support of the writing of this book.

1 The basics of sport sponsorship

Sponsorship – a 20-year juggernaut

Sponsorship, like much of marketing and the business world in general, was on a sustained positive growth curve from the late 1990s to the end of 2019. In fact, during this time, sponsorship outpaced most other areas of marketing. It even withstood, if not thrived, during the Great Recession of 2007–2009 that impacted most parts of the world. A study of the professional sport business, including sponsorship, around this recession, found no major impacts of the Great Recession (Humphreys, 2010).

Back then, coming out of the recession, we, like many, spoke about sponsorship being "recession proof" or viewed it as being on an ever-increasing growth curve, able to withstand larger economic trends. Research that we undertook, at the time, even showed that in some contexts sponsorship investment actually increased during the recession.

This positive growth continued throughout the entire 2010–2019 decade.

Describing sponsorship as a 21st-century juggernaut, although perhaps an exaggeration, would be an apt way to describe the field's growth until 2019. For instance, the United States based agency IEG, in its annual sponsorship report, has estimated that global sponsorship spending has more than tripled from just over USD$20 billion in 2000 to close to USD$70 billion prior to the onset of COVID-19 in early 2020. In Canada, the Canadian Sponsorship Landscape Study (2020) has estimated that the spending more than doubled from 2006 to 2019, reaching CDN$3.15 billion in 2019. Similarly, IEG estimated that North American sponsorship spending more than doubled from about USD$11 billion in 2004 to more than USD$25 billion before the COVID-19 pandemic. See Figure 1.1 for a depiction of the global sponsorship trends and an illustration of its growth.

DOI: 10.4324/9781003154631-1

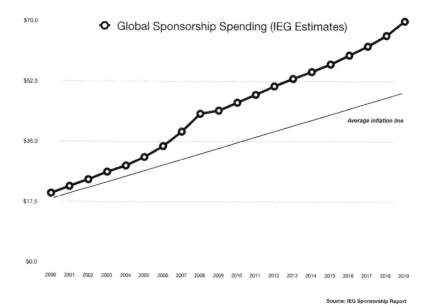

Figure 1.1 Global Sponsorship Spending.
Source: IEG Sponsorship Report, chart created by authors.

To put this into context, the earliest known global sponsorship spending estimate was done in 1982, with USD$500 million as the projection (Kuzma & Shanklin, 1994) of sponsorship rights fee spend in 1982. A quick calculation finds a more than 140-fold increase in just the 37 years that follows to 2019. By comparison, inflation in the North America during that same 37-year time period is about an increase of a factor of 2.8. In simpler terms, the purchasing power of $1.00 in 1982 is about the same as $2.80 in 2019.

For comparison, this average inflation line is also included in Figure 1.1.

So, based on this data, maybe juggernaut is not an exaggeration after all.

But, much like how the Marvel uber-villain Juggernaut was stopped in his tracks by hero Colossus in the film Deadpool 2, sponsorship was derailed in early 2020. The COVID-19 global pandemic of 2020 and 2021 did the derailing. Yes, sponsorship, like any business function, was impacted globally by the virus that left no country, no industry, and no activity alone.

The point of starting off the book with these points is not to dissuade you from reading further or to be negative. Quite the contrary, we have done so explicitly to describe how effective sponsorship can be in certain situations and to set up what it will look like – and what you need to be prepared for as a sponsorship professional – in the future.

AUTHORS' BLOG: THE PASSION PODIUM

When you were young, did you dream of being a star athlete? Or a legendary coach? Perhaps you wanted to be a sideline reporter? A team general manager? Or even a team owner?

In all of those dreams, we bet you never imagined the opportunity to be a sponsorship marketer. If you were like us, you probably did not know that such a career existed. At least, it might not have been until you were well past the age when you realized the Olympics, the Masters, Wimbledon, the Final Four, and the Monaco Grand Prix were all beyond your athletic potential.

You may not be able to jump as high as you hoped, but you will be able to reach dizzying heights by becoming a sponsorship marketer. Your speed will not limit your potential in the 40-yard dash. The significant part of becoming a sponsorship marketer is that the attributes you need do not include speed, strength, and stamina.

There is only one prerequisite – PASSION.

Passion will take you to the podium and back in sponsorship marketing.

We can attest to you that passion is the most important attribute that we seek in people we partner with as associates. We want it in our friends, our colleagues, our clients, and even our families. We want it to ooze out of everything we do. To ensure that, it must ooze out of you.

The sponsorship marketing industry is overflowing with passion.

Every business can create a diverse culture where passion, purpose, and profit live in perfect balance. To achieve this balance is predicated entirely on the people who make up that business.

Passion is mandatory because you need the conviction to succeed, the devotion to your craft, and the desire to excel in everyone's organization. The purpose is critical in business because your customers, followers, fans, participants, volunteers, and followers need to understand why you exist before they subscribe to your offering. Profit is mandatory, even in a not-for-profit, because financial freedom is necessary for an organization to choose its path.

You cannot sustain long-term profits or stay focused on your purpose unless you have passionate people. It is easy to be passionate about the sponsorship business. From a corporate standpoint, you have an opportunity to drive the success of brands, leagues, teams, media outlets, vendors, and suppliers. From a societal perspective, you have a chance to make the world a healthier place to live, to build a community that comes from being involved with an event, and to unlock potential by providing opportunities for volunteers to learn new skills. For many people in our sector, passion comes from the fandom for the sport. For others, it comes from the creativity our industry provides. Still for others, it is the breadth of exposure from being involved with dozens of touchpoints from advertising to digital, to merchandising, to social media, to events, to experiences, to publicity.

Mark, the chief executive officer (CEO) among the authors, describes his passion as both very selfish and very public. He loves nothing more than being a connector of people. He loves networking. He loves meeting new people. He loves connecting the dots.

Sponsorship marketers get this opportunity more than any other form of marketing. There are multitudes of players involved in every deal, from team executives to marketing agencies to government officials to broadcasters to influencers to volunteers. Our industry has a unique and powerful bond. That bond is interdependence.

In sponsorship marketing, you cannot just press a button or issue some cryptocurrency or turn on a spotlight and expect that your program will come to life. No, you have to marshal all sorts of people into a tribe aligned with a vision and understanding of what is to be accomplished to succeed. There is a tremendous amount of opportunity for human error in sponsorship marketing, making the challenge all the more stimulating.

It is not a cliché to say that sponsorship marketing is the most fantastic team sport globally. Like any good team, you need all the right pieces, the proper preparation, and the right strategy. You need the superstars, and you need the glue. It would help if you had a coach who says the right thing at the right time. It would help if you had a bit of luck and much perseverance.

In the end, if you are a person who wants to have still dreamed of sporting glory beyond the age of 30, unless you are Tom Brady or Lionel Messi, the sponsorship marketing world is for you. Not only is it a world where you can dream, but it is a world that provides you with the tools to make your dreams come true.

Sponsorship's current reality and future: a dozen observations

In order to provide valuable insights about sponsorship, there are a series of 12 key observations that we want to share that occurred over the course of the pandemic that – in our view – will have both positive and negative impacts on sponsorship in the future. Many others will follow throughout the book, but this set of insights is the key one in illustrating the current reality of sponsorship and providing the foundation for the future of sponsorship.

1 **Confirmation that sponsorship works**: Let us start with a positive one. We knew this already (much more detail on this later in this chapter), but the pandemic showed us again that sponsorship, if done right, does work. And it can work very well. For a sponsor with objectives related to brand equity, image transfer, and intellectual property, sponsorship is shown to be superior in most contexts to other promotional tactics such as advertising, personal sales, sales promotion, and public relations. Now, you might be asking what some of the branding terms mean or represent in sponsorship, so let us briefly explain each.

   a Sponsorship objective(s) – what a brand wants to achieve out of its investment in a sponsorship property. This includes, among others, the following.

      i Brand equity – it is a mental image, perception, or impression that people have of a brand. In other words, it is what people think of or the impression people have of a brand at the moment they encounter it. It is the (dis)likeness and the commercial value of the name, mark, and images of a commercial entity. For example, the Nike brand is reported to be worth more than the Puma in sport apparel brands. Sponsorship can enhance the equity of a brand, which is what Puma sought to do with their long-term sponsorship of sprint legend Usain Bolt (*Marketing Week*, 2010). The Adidas and Boca Juniors experience, Case Study 1.1, provides a deeper example of brand equity enhancement as a sponsorship objective.

Case study 1.1 Adiheadas and Boca Juniors[1]

After 23 years with the Nike Swoosh on their jerseys, the Argentinian football club Boca Juniors signed a ten-year, USD$100 million+ deal with Adidas, effective January 2020. This deal made the German apparel brand the new kit supplier of the South American football superpower. The deal, reportedly worth a club record USD$10 million per year, also saw Boca receiving a USD$3 million signing bonus. Boca also received all royalty income from shirt sales, both nationally and abroad, an agreement within the contract that no other South American football club was able to gain in their deals. This deal also one-upped Boca's rival, River Plate, that holds an apparel sponsorship with Adidas of USD$6.5 million. Adidas reportedly initially put forward a five-year contract, with Nike offering an extension to their existing deal for ten years, but for less money. Adidas previously supplied Boca's kit from 1979 to 1993.

In addition to the sheer scope of the deal, there were multiple other economic benefits for Boca. First, Boca would receive USD$90,000 per year to be used for investment in different marketing campaigns. Also, Adidas would be responsible for developing a women's clothing line, children's clothing line, and lifestyle items, in addition to the men's clothing line. Finally, Adidas also offered Boca fixed amount bonuses in the case of local and international titles, with the potential for these amounts to be updated.

The deal with Adidas was officially announced on January 10th, 2020 through a video on the social media accounts of the football club. Prior to the announcement, photos of the new kit had leaked online.

ii   Image transfer – this is a well-established reason why sponsorship works (Gwinner & Eaton, 1999). Image transfer refers the practice of transferring a culturally acquired perceived quality of an entity (e.g., a sport property) onto a brand (e.g., a sponsor) (McCracken, 1989). The image that is transferred onto the brand through sponsorship is then expected to produce a favorable image of the brand in the minds of consumers.

iii Intellectual Property – this refers to an intangible asset with a great financial value. It may include copyrights (designs, drawings) and trademarks (any word, name, symbol, or combination of them representing a property).

The most evident example are the Olympic Games, which includes the Olympic logo, Olympic emblems, the Olympic flag, the Olympic torch, and the Olympic anthem.

b Promotional Tactics – in marketing strategy, there are traditionally four elements, known as "The 4 P's", which frame strategic thinking in marketing. One of these P's is promotions. Promotions refer to a set of activities which communicate a brand (product, service, or idea) to consumers (Shank & Lyberger, 2014). It is, simply, communicating with or to customers. At times, it is referred to as marketing communication. The tactical elements of the promotion mix refer to the blend of promotional elements used to communicate to or with consumers. These include advertising (e.g., signage, website banner, TV commercial), personal sales (e.g., sales agents selling a product in one-on-one dialogue), publicity (e.g., paid promotional space in a news outlet, such as a glob), sales promotions (e.g., discounts, buy one and get one free), public relations (e.g., building a basketball court in an underprivileged neighborhood), and sponsorship.

2 **Sponsorship and the COVID-19 pandemic.** During the pandemic, the fact that sponsorship works was readily observable in the widespread loss of sponsorship when live events were largely shut down (no fans in venues, no in-person connection to athletes, etc.), leading to the rise of digital sponsorship assets as sponsors altered their sponsorship investments to include helmet sponsorships, jersey sponsorships, gambling, esports, and fantasy sports.

2.1 Sponsorship investments by brands cut in half. Estimates vary, but a common theme is that about half of the planned dollars have come out of sponsorship in 2020 and 2021. A set of global studies (mostly a North American sample) with four waves in 2020 by SponsorshipX surveyed sponsors (brands) who estimated a decrease in rights fee investment of 37% and activation spend of 46% versus what they had originally planned for 2020 due to COVD-19. A couple of additional explanations of terms is due here as you learn sponsorship:

a Rights fee investment – the amount a brand pays a sport property to have an official right of association with the sport property.

b   Activation – the additional investment beyond the rights fee to execute different marketing communication efforts and other activities (e.g., hospitality) to support the sponsorship and enhance its effectiveness.

2.2 Major professional and Olympic sport held steady. As noted in insight 2.1 above, the pandemic led to a loss of investment in sport by brands, but that loss was disproportionately felt in all of sports outside of the major professional sport leagues and the Olympic committees. In other words, major sport properties largely held, and in some cases, improved their sponsorship situations. In North America, for instance, the National Football League (NFL) and Major League Baseball (MLB) were able to hold their regular seasons – with limited or no fans in venue in 2020 and 2021, while the National Basketball Association (NBA) and National Hockey League (NHL) finished their 2019–2020 seasons in successful "bubbles" (i.e., isolated, centralized venues with all clubs playing one or two locations) and played in shortened 2020–2021 seasons in closed venues or in front of fewer fans. In Europe, the same story resulted for the five major premier leagues (England, Spain, Italy, France, and Germany) and the UEFA Champions League, with games being played in venues without fans in attendance. Major individual sports (tennis, golf, and auto racing) had a few cancelled events (e.g., Wimbledon 2020, 2020 Australian Grand Prix), but were able to carry on, in most cases, with empty (or low capacity) venues. At the Olympic Level, the 2020 Tokyo Games were delayed for a year, but most Games-related sponsorship (international and national) were extended for a year to accommodate. In the summer of 2021, the Games happened but in a bubble format without fans in most venues. In sum, for all of these major sport properties, sponsorship was impacted by no live event activations, but reductions, from our knowledge, were modest at best, with activations often changed from live to digital (e.g., esports, social media content) with no (or modest) reductions in rights fees.

2.3 The individual elite athlete as a sponsored property. The pandemic has validated the growing reach and importance of individual elite athletes in sponsorship. They are influencers, celebrities, ambassadors, social justice champions, role models, and sources of data via their social media channels. It is important to note that only the most elite and highest reaching of these athletes will attract brand interests but those who do – Naomi Osaka, Cristiano Ronaldo, LeBron James, Lionel Messi, Novak Djokovic, Michael Jordan, and their fellow superstars – will become highly valuable sponsorable properties, perhaps more so than the clubs, countries, and/or events they compete for/in. Elite athletes are often attractive to sponsors due to their star status and the emotional attachment that fans form with them, which, in turn, gives them the power to influence attitudes, particularly in those fans who admire and identify themselves with the athlete, which can be activated to stimulate purchase intention.

2.4 Minor professional sport, grassroots sport, youth sport, and collegiate/university sport seasons cancelled. This is a polar opposite story of insights 2.2 and 2.3 above. Counter to major sports maintaining much of their sponsorship investments, the rest of the sport was hit very hard, with seasons cancelled, games withdrawn, championships postponed, staff laid off or furloughed, budgets cut, and so on. In many cases, sponsors honored their 2020 rights fee commitments by either asking for digital assets in return for the lost live event ones or accepting that the contract was already in place and thereby not asking for a refund. Of course, in either scenario, activation spend was cancelled or drastically reduced when an event did not happen. As the pandemic moved into its second year, 2021, if a sport property had not been able to find a way to operate (either live or digital), we observed that interest in continuing to invest as a sponsor was much lower.

2.5 Digital assets are the way forward. The aforementioned SponsorshipX studies reported that the number one piece of advice from sponsorship industry professionals to smaller or minor properties during the pandemic was not to pivot or change, but to wait and invest in digital assets. Yes, hundreds of sponsorship industry experts advised those properties who are struggling in the pandemic to buckle down, save where they can, avoid making rash changes that are not authentic, and invest into new assets that would have value to sponsors and that would integrate digital component. Augmented reality, virtual reality, and artificial intelligence are all part of these digital assets. It is time to invest, to create, to innovate, and to build.

2.6 Live events sponsorship will return. It may be a while and it will likely be different than before, and perhaps smaller or more controlled, but many studies have shown that people – on all corners of the globe – want to travel, to go to a restaurant with friends, to go on a date, to have a party, to attend a sport event, and to go to the movies. However, they only want to do so, if they can do so safely, and this a very big caveat. This knowledge equips sponsorship professionals with the insight that safety of participants, support of front-line workers, and the creation of safe live experiences are all sponsorship opportunities of the future.

3   **Generational shifts matter.** Just ask anyone in golf, cricket, or baseball if age is an issue for their sport. Although the vast majority of the Lost Generation (over 76 years of age in 2021), baby boomers (57–75 years), and Gen Xers (41–56) devote a significant proportion of their free time and discretionary resources to participating in and spectating sport, the younger generations (i.e., Millennials (25–40), Gen Z (11–24), and Gen Alpha (10 and under) are relatively less interested in sport. Now, there are exceptions to this, namely, esports, NBA, fantasy sport, sport gambling, and sport-based video games. The implications to sponsorship vary by generation and by sport. And, perhaps most importantly, there is vast uncertainty about what Gen Z and Gen Alpha folks will be like as adults, but we know that their habits, interests, and qualities are very different from any generation before.

And you may ask, Why will they be so different?

In response, experts agree on a few key reasons why we need to view these two generations (Gen Z and Gen Alpha) as different, namely (i) they have an attention span of less than ten seconds; (ii) they are technology natives, that is technology is inherent to all that they do in life; (iii) television is not the ideal way for them to consume sport; in fact, streaming and social media are the dominant forms; (iv) the environment and the planet are more important to them than previous generations; (v) they have a distaste for overt marketing and overt advertising (i.e., paying for things they do not need); (vi) experiences are what they seek; and (vii) they have a global perspective. One could combine (vi) and (vii) and say global experiences. An insight specific to the pandemic is that these generations have lost many opportunities for experiences, potentially setting the stage for a future boom in this regard.

4   **Data analysis with storytelling enabled.** The data revolution in sport started with *Moneyball* and Sabermetrics in the 1990s to inform on-the-field decisions in sport, and today has moved to the off-the-field side, the business side, including sponsorship.

a *Moneyball* (author: Michael Lewis) is a landmark book that first exposed the cutting-edge work of Oakland Athletics general manager Billy Beane to use analytics over scouting in evaluating players for his MLB club.

b Sabermetrics refers to using or applying mathematics or statistics to, first, baseball, and now any sport data, as a means to improve on-field performance, player evaluation, and coaching decisions.

But data is not enough in sponsorship; it needs to tell a story. An effective sponsorship professional today needs to know how to analyze and then turn the result into a story. Importantly, a sponsorship professional must have skills in data gathering, digital data acquisition, and data analysis, which is crucial to understand the sport fan. Thus, quality data, intelligently analyzed and well packaged, has been further supported as a key to successful sponsorship. Big data (e.g., digital data) allows marketers to understand the customers of a sport property (e.g., demography, psychography, geography) and thereby customize marketing approaches that appeal to a specific market segment, which, in turn, allows a sponsorship message to efficiently reach a targeted market segment.

5 **The diverse nature of "Return-on-Sponsorship" expands**. Sponsorship is a business activity and one that seeks to justify itself by generating a return for the sponsor in excess of the investment made (rights fees plus activation). Over the course of the chapters that follow, you will learn – among other things – how to activate, to service, to valuate, and to evaluate a sponsorship. These are tactics designed to help a brand maximize its ROI (return on investment), which we will call return on objective (ROO) to describe what many practitioners call return on sponsorship, or the ability of a sponsorship to achieve the objectives set out for the sponsorship. ROO can take many forms, including the traditionally sought outcomes of awareness, sales, image transfer, and relationship building, but also some more modern outcomes related to experiences, social change, environmental impact, and social responsibility. ROO differs from sponsorship to sponsorship and is based on the relevant sponsorship objectives of the brand as the sponsoring party.

6 **The gap is widening between the haves and have-nots**. A key insight that COVID has accelerated is the sponsorship gap (that has been happening already) between major properties who have digital

reach and digital assets versus all those properties that do not. Specifically, this means that major properties with vast global reach will outpace smaller regional properties with limited reach. Further, it suggests that global events, multicountry properties, and digital-only properties will thrive in sponsorship in the future.

7 **The continuation of festivalization.** We were one of the first to bring the term "festivalization" to sponsorship nearly a decade ago and it is more relevant than ever today. The Super Bowl and Olympic Games remain the gold standards for integrating entertainment into a sport property to "festivalize" it for sponsorship outcomes. Music festivals and major art shows have known this for decades, but small sport properties are only starting to grasp this insight. In the new era of sponsorship, where events will be both traditional and digital in nature (i.e., hybrid), creating a festival like event for small properties will become increasingly challenging. For instance, a 5 km run can expand their offering to include a 1 km kids run, a pre-event pasta party, a postevent awards ceremony with a concert, and other ancillary events over the entirety of a weekend.

Figure 1.2 summarizes the current reality and future of sponsorship as discussed above.

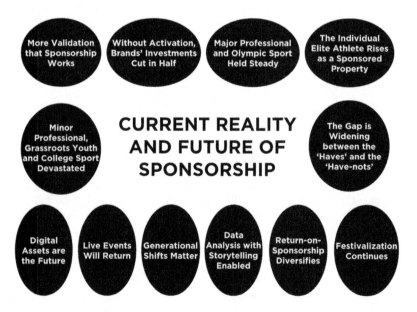

Figure 1.2 Current Reality and Future of Sponsorship.

Sponsorship in marketing

As you may have gathered from some of the commentary around the current trends in sponsorship, it is – typically and traditionally – viewed to sit as one of the key elements of the promotional mix (along with advertising, publicity, personal sales, sales promotion, and public relations) within the marketing mix (the 4 Ps – product, price, place, and promotion). For those who like a clear delineated view of marketing, this makes a lot of sense.

Let us explain. Assume you are a marketing manager of a company that is considering becoming the title sponsor of an upcoming World Championship in the city where your firm is headquartered. You have done your research on the event and are now working with your team to decide if you want to enter into the agreement that they have offered you. You are a sponsor, so you must ask yourself, "What do we (as the sponsor) want?" Yes, what is in it for you. You start by going back to your marketing plan and asking if this sponsorship fits with the marketing objectives you have set and if it will allow you to reach the customers you need to reach. Does the event attract spectators, participants, volunteers, and other stakeholders who are your target markets?

Let us assume that you answered yes to these questions and that the event can help you achieve your marketing goals. Next, you move to the promotional mix and assess how this sponsorship can fit with your advertising, digital, web, publicity, PR (public relations), and sales promotions planned. You are also aware that these can be achieved through in-person communication or through the four major communication mediums: electronics (TV, radio), print (newspapers, magazines), outdoor (billboards, posters, fliers), and online (website, social media, and other digital such as AR and VR). Can you integrate the different elements of promotional mix? Can you activate the sponsorship through other activities? Can you link sales promotions to be timed around the sponsorship? Can you leverage the sponsorship to drive potential customers to your website and social channels?

We assume that you likely got the point by now. The point is that sponsorship is an important tactical element in the marketing tool kit of brands, alongside the other elements of its promotional mix and its overall marketing strategy (e.g., product, price, place).

If the 4 P's and the promotional mix are traditional marketing, then the concept of "sponsorship-linked marketing" (Cornwell et al., 2005), which we will explain in much more detail in later chapters, is what we would recommend you keep in mind as you learn sponsorship and put it into practice. Sponsorship-linked marketing, as proposed by Cornwell and her colleagues, frames sponsorship as an essential part of the promotions that brands undertake, but powerfully links sponsorship to marketing, seeking cognitive (e.g., awareness of brand, product, service), affective (e.g., consumer preference), and behavioral (e.g., purchase) outcomes from the sponsorship that is deeply engrained in the brand's overall marketing efforts and processed based on the attributes/value of the sponsored property.

Why study sport sponsorship

One of the basic foundations of this book, as noted earlier, and a core pillar on which we will build the chapters that follow is that, when done right, sponsorship works, and it works well. There are lots of academic and industry research to support this, and our collective academic and industry experiences put us in strong agreement. In fact, the content of Chapter 5 will establish this clearly and, more importantly, share with you a set of evaluation tools that you can use to figure out for yourself if and how sport sponsorship works.

But do not just take our word for it. Why does it work?

There are a few core reasons.

First, as briefly introduced earlier in the chapter, sponsorship can transfer image through the right partnership fit and effective activation. For instance, the sport drink Gatorade – the PepsiCo-owned market leader in its category for more than 30 years – has much of its success built on sponsorships that transferred images from sport properties to the brand. Whether it was the Florida Gators football team, the Hawaiian Ironman triathlon, or the NHL, the brand's ongoing sponsorships (as well as a quality product that delivers on its brand promise) have transferred the images of "endurance", "sweat", "hydration", "thirst quencher", and others from the properties to Gatorade, making it the market leader for energy drinks in North America. Gatorade also executes innovative activations such as the Gatorade Sport Science Institute and the Gatorade Sweat Test, all designed to transfer the images of "sweat", "dehydration", and "endurance" to Gatorade as the solution for athletes seeking performance in physically demanding sport.

During the COVID-19 global pandemic, Gatorade's usage increased in North America and its market share held, even in the face of tough competition from Powerade (Coca-Cola owned and lower priced) and fast-rising BODYARMOR (cool upstart newer brand with many athlete endorsers). Much like Gatorade, both Powerade and

BODYARMOR use sponsorships as a significant part of their market-ing efforts, including sponsoring athletes, leagues, clubs, and events. Second, sponsorship provides the ability to reach target markets in a "clean way". By clean we mean that there are no competitors (of the sponsor) in sight. For instance, during the Olympic Games, when any Olympic sponsor is showcasing its product or its brands, its competi-tors will not be allowed to promote their brand anywhere where a fan or viewer could potentially see them. Coca-Cola and VISA, for instance, have clean presentation without Pepsi, Mastercard, or American Ex-press allowed. The nonsponsors do not have the right to associate with the Olympic rings, the Games, or any associated images. In sponsor-ship terminology, this is known as "exclusivity", which is something properties typically provide and guarantee for their sponsors.

Third, activation (as described earlier) is something that differen-tiates sponsorship from other promotional activities, particularly ad-vertising. Activation can take many forms, for example, in a standard activation (e.g., the CEO of a sponsoring company drops the puck at the start of the hockey game) or an innovative one (e.g., a telecom sponsor AT&T and the Dallas Cowboys partnering to enhance fans' experience using an augmented reality (AR) photo opportunity en-titled "Pose with the Pros"). In both cases, an investment is made in addition to the rights fee investment to leverage the sponsorship to achieve the preestablished objectives that the brand has set out for the sponsorship.

Fourth, as sponsorship has continued to grow, senior executives at brands (chief financial officers (CFOs), chief marketing officers (CMOs), etc.) have been increasingly asking for justification of their investments. Both the industry and the scholarly communities have responded, and evidence has been produced to its effectiveness. For example, global research firm IMI International (2021) report on a US-based study that found that 39% of Americans purchased the product or service of a brand because they sponsored a sport, cause, cultural, or music event that they follow. While an agreement exists that sponsorship works, corporate sponsors are increasingly looking for greater precision regarding a return on their increased sponsorship investment, meaning that marketers are challenged to justify sponsor-ship spending with evidence.

Fifth, sponsorship is established to be a tool that allows marketers to cut through the enormous amount of "clutter" that people are exposed to on a daily basis both in traditional mediums (e.g., signage, radio, print) and – increasingly – digital content (e.g., web, social, mobile).

The ability to associate to a sport property could mean a competitor-free way that provides the ability to "break through" and capture the target audience's attention. Case study 1.2 below on Sleep Number and the NFL provides an example of a sponsorship that allows a manufacturer of smart beds to cut through the clutter and differentiate itself from their competitors' offerings.

Case study 1.2   Sleep Number and NFL[2]

In 2018, the NFLPA and Sleep Number announced a sponsorship partnership through the NFLPA licensing and marketing division, NFL Players Inc. The sponsorship included the provision of a Sleep Number 360 Smart Bed to every active NFL player, more than 1,600 beds (approximate retail value USD$2,000). The use of the SleepIQ Technology allows player comfort to be evaluated throughout the night, additionally collecting data such as average breathing and heart rate. This data, in turn, has been used in modifying player performance and recovery, leading to "holistic advances in player well-being". Gina Scott, vice president, Partner Services, NFLPA, cited the partnership as the league's investment in "[valuing] the impact of quality sleep on performance and recovery." While an exact value of the sponsorship was not provided, a source cited the deal as a minimum of three years and in the "high seven figures per year".

In an interview between Evan Vladem (sports marketing consultant) and Kevin Brown (Sleep Number CMO) in 2019, the following important points were reported. First, the NFL was targeted by Sleep Number due to its large marketing platforms which overlap with Sleep Number's target audience (consumers 35–64 years old), and because the partnership could help them "break out from the clutter" of bed providers. Second, Sleep Number launched a four-part content series in line with the 2019 NFL Draft to showcase the impact of quality sleep on NFL draftees. This effort was undertaken to connect with consumers based on emotion and connection to the NFL, rather than just the "awesome features, functions, and benefits" of the bed. Third, Sleep Number measures its brand three times a year using various metrics, and the partnership "significantly moved our buzz metric and our word-of-mouth metric".

Finally, in looking at the United States, where sponsorship is arguably the most developed, there is some evidence of its success that can be extended to other contexts. This provides the sixth and seventh points about why sponsorship works. Sixth, high school sport and collegiate sports in United States are major sponsored properties, given their ability to reach local communities, students, faculty, staff, and alumni of the given educational institution. In Canada, the support of minor sport, particularly youth ice hockey, is demonstrated in Case study 1.3.

Case study 1.3 Tim Hortons and Hockey Canada[3]

Anyone who has played amateur hockey in Canada is familiar with early mornings at the rink. And if you've driven yourself or your child to the rink early in the morning, you've likely had a coffee along the way or from the concession stand. Beyond the brand being named after a hockey great, Tim Hortons and hockey in Canada often appear joined at the hip, and the two entities have embraced it. Over the years, Tim Hortons has sponsored numerous activations with Hockey Canada, including Timbits Hockey, Upper Deck Tim Hortons Hockey cards, and numerous player promotions such as Jump the Boards with Sidney Crosby. The restaurant giant has also been a premier sponsor of multiple Hockey Canada events, including the Centennial Cup and the IIHF World Junior Championship. As "an iconic Canadian brand with deep roots in the hockey community", in the words of Mike Ross, chief business development officer, Tim Hortons signed a four-year deal with Hockey Canada in 2018. With a philosophy not based on winning or losing, but on learning new sports, Tim Hortons provides opportunities for more than 100,000 children aged four to eight in house league sports across Canada, with their logo placed on the chest of each of them. With advertising like this, it's no wonder a Tim Hortons coffee can be seen in the hands of nearly every parent in the stands.

Seventh, sponsorship thrives in urban environments, where large numbers of target markets and numerous activation opportunities exist. The United States, as of 2021, has more than 300 cities with populations in excess of 100,000 people.[4] This large and developed urban

Figure 1.3 Rationales for Sponsorship Effectiveness.

lifestyle – in nonpandemic times – is ideal for many sponsorship activations in venues where large numbers of potential customers can be reached.

Figure 1.3 summarizes this section and our seven reasons why to study sponsorship and, more specifically, why sponsorship works.

Notes

1 https://www.sportspromedia.com/news/boca-juniors-nike-adidas-100-million-new-kit-deal; https://sgbonline.com/adidas-to-sponsor-boca-juniors/; https://sponsorship.sportbusiness.com/news/adidas-to-replace-nike-as-boca-juniors-partner/; https://www.nssmag.com/en/sports/20483/adidas-boca-juniors-official

2 https://nflpa.com/partners/posts/more-than-1-600-nfl-players-using-sleep-data-and-the-sleep-number-360-smart-bed-to-enhance-on-and-off-field-performance; https://www.honestmattressreviews.com/sleep-number-nfl/; https://www.chiefmarketer.com/is-the-sleep-number-smart-bed-the-top-pick-of-the-NFL-draft/; https://opendorse.com/blog/what-is-a-sponsorship-activation/

3 https://www.hockeycanada.ca/en-ca/news/partners-tims-expands-partnership; https://www.hockeycanada.ca/en-ca/news/2018-coach-new-partnership-with-tims; https://www.hockeycanada.ca/en-ca/hockey-programs/coaching/under-7/timbits-jerseys; https://www.insidethegames.biz/articles/1088313/hockey-canada-tim-hortons-marketing

4 https://worldpopulationreview.com/us-cities

References

Canadian Sponsorship Landscape Study (2020). 14th annual report. www. sponsorshiplandscape.ca.

Cornwell, T.B., Weeks, C.S., & Roy, D.P. (2005). Sponsorship-linked marketing: Opening the black box. *Journal of Advertising, 34*(2), 21–42.

Gwinner, K., & Eaton, J. (1999). Building brand image through event sponsorship: The role of image transfer. *Journal of Advertising, 28*(4), 47–57.

Humphreys, B.R. (2010). The impact of the global financial crisis on sport in North America. In S. Butenko, J. Gil-Lafuente, & P.M. Pardalos (Eds.), *Optimal strategies in sports economics and management* (pp. 39–57). Berlin: Springer.

IEG Sponsorship Report (various years). https://www.sponsorship.com/ Report.aspx

IMI International (2021). https://www.consultimi.com/sponsorpulse/

Kuzma, J.R., & Shanklin, W.L. (1994). Corporate sponsorship: An application for analysis. In P.J. Graham (Ed.), *Sport business, operational and theoretical aspects* (pp. 82–87). Madison, WI: Brown and Benchmark.

Marketing Week (2010). https://www.marketingweek.com/usain-bolt-signs-largest-ever-athletics-deal-with-puma/

McCracken, G. (1989). Who is the celebrity endorser? Cultural foundations of the endorsement process. *Journal of Consumer Research, 16*(3), 310–321.

Shank, M.D., & Lyberger, M.R. (2014). *Sports marketing: A strategic perspective*. Abingdon: Routledge.

2 Sponsorship objectives, stakeholders, proposals, and packages

The foundation of sport sponsorship is charitable giving, and up until the 1970s, sponsorship was no different from any other philanthropic donation. Often, a brand entered into a sponsorship based on the individual interests of senior management, rather than a careful assessment of the sponsorship benefits for the organization. The adage went like this: "the CEO, well, she likes to golf, so we're sponsoring golf".

However, with the advancement of electronic media and the expansion of advertising practice in the 1980s and early 1990s, sport sponsorship started to be viewed as an alternative to advertising and as a way of obtaining media exposure (Crompton, 2004). In the early 1980s, companies started investing sizeable resources in global sponsorship (Mullin et al., 2007), reaching a projected USD$500 million in spending in 1982 (Kuzma & Shanklin, 1994). As shown in Figure 1.1 in Chapter 1, IEG reports ongoing, consistent growth in global sponsorship spending up to 2019, with estimates approaching USD$70 billion in global spending prior to COVID-19.

Over the years, sport has received the lion's share of total global sponsorship investment. Other property types that attract sponsorship include festivals, arts, municipalities, causes, culture, entertainment, associations, parks, and annual events. By most accounts and public reports, sport attracts between a 50% and 75% share of sponsorship investment in most countries. Many sport properties (e.g., events, athletes, facilities, teams, leagues, federations) are attractive to sponsors because they provide a highly involved, passionate, and loyal audience that comprises individuals (spectators or participants) with common characteristics in terms of demography, psychographics, and geography. As you may ask what these terms refer to, here's a quickly explanation.

DOI: 10.4324/9781003154631-2

- Demography – the social characteristics of the population or sample of interest, including variables such as gender, birth rate, marriage, population, and age.
- Psychographics – the internal characteristics of a population such as their attitudes, interests, and tastes.
- Geography – the details of where the population of interest lives, such as country, rural/urban/suburban, terrain, and housing.

In addition to these characteristics, sponsorship targets can also be assessed by the features of involvement and commitment (emotional attachment). Here's a brief explanation about each of these.

- Involvement – how engaged a fan or participant is in a sport property. For example, a season ticket holder versus a one-time single game purchaser, or a member of a golf club versus a one-time player.
- Commitment – the level of engagement of an individual in the sport property. To illustrate, a highly committed die-hard fan lives and breathes their favorite team and spends most of their discretionary time and income on activities related to that team. Commitment is sometimes referred to as emotional attachment to the club or sport.

Sports that have a sufficient group of fans and/or participants who are involved and committed, and have demographic, psychographic, and geographic characteristics that a brand seeks, can lead to them being an ideal platform for successful sponsorship.

You may ask why sport is any different than the sponsorship of other properties.

Let us explain using and building on the seminal research work of Copeland et al. (1996), who discussed four attributes of sport that attract corporate sponsors. First, specific target groups can be reached in a more direct and cost-efficient manner. In the many years since their work, this is characterized by a sport property's ability to help a brand reach its target markets. This can be achieved by connecting to the fans/participants of that sport with the involved and committed segments whose demographic, psychographic, and geographic characteristics match those of the sponsor's consumers. Case study 2.1 below provides an illustration of the ability of a sport property (in this case an esports team) to provide a brand (Apple's Beats by Dre) the ability to connect with their sought-after target markets, their likely objective for the sponsorship.

Case study 2.1 Beats by Dre and League of Legends TOP Esports and FaZe Clan[1]

While Bose is an official sponsor of Riot Games, TOP Esports, a Chinese esports organization, signed a deal with Apple's Beats by Dre in 2020. Despite the team being unable to wear Beats headphones during competitions due to Riot Games' deal with Bose, the team will wear the Beats logo on the right shoulder of their jerseys. Although the financial terms of the agreement were not disclosed when the partnership was announced, Beats became the sixth official sponsor of the team, joining Logitech G, Audi, and more. This partnership came after the onset of the pandemic, and the temporary shutdown of the NBA, causing Beats to look for a new entity to sponsor. The addition of Beats, backed by the tech giant Apple, is a good sign for the world of esports as more reputable brands begin to get involved in the competitive video gaming space.

Since the deal, Beats also released a special-edition FaZe Clan-branded wireless headphone set. The limited-edition run included FaZe's signature red tiger camouflage, and the sale of the headphones through a lottery system facilitated by e-commerce marketplace NTWRK. This partnership symbolizes the collaboration between the music and video gaming worlds, and, similar to the partnership with TOP Esports, furthers esport credibility with major brands.

Second, Copeland et al. (1996) noted that the image of a sponsor can be enhanced as a company associates itself with the positive features of a sport product. You may recall the Gatorade example from Chapter 1. This is one of the true value points of a sport property in sponsorship, namely, that it possesses images that a sponsor seeks and can, in turn, transfer – in the minds of consumers – through effective activation. Case study 2.2 helps illustrate this point, where the South African telecom company MTN used its sponsorship of the Springboks, the leading sport property in South Africa and the country's national rugby team, to transfer the positive national images of the team to South African rugby fans and beyond.

Case study 2.2 MTN and Springboks[2]

Everyone loves being associated with a winner, but MTN, the South African telecom company, stresses that the negotiation to extend its sponsorship with the Springboks began prior to their World Cup win in 2019. The previous three-year deal, from 2017 to 2019, was reportedly worth more than USD$2.7 million per year, and included branding on the front of the Springboks jersey in all competitive matches, aside from the Rugby World Cup. The deal was announced on Day 1 of the teams four-day Trophy Tour following the World Cup win, although an MTN executive stressed that the deal would have been made regardless of whether the Springboks won or lost. "The reason being that we have seen how this sponsorship, from a national perspective, has absolutely brought people together" (in the words of Jacqui O'Sullivan, MTN SA's corporate affairs executive). The partnership between the two is a story of succeeding together. When the Springboks approached MTN in 2017, they were struggling both on and off the pitch, "really battling to get a corporate sponsor."

Since the original deal, the sponsorship has paid off for both parties. Over the years, numerous sponsorship activations have been initiated. In 2018, MTN and Springboks began the "Be the 'Bozza'" social media activation, rewarding three fans with front row seats whenever the Springboks play. In 2019, MTN initiated the "WeGotU, Bokke" campaign, supporting the Springboks on their way to the 2019 Rugby World Cup, and sending a few lucky fans to the championship as well. These types of activations have created a culture of support and success within South African rugby, uniting the nation behind its national team.

Next, Copeland et al. (1996) suggested that sport often generates substantial excitement and emotional attachment among its consumers, and that such an attachment may lead to better reach of sponsors' messages and activations. Since then, this dynamic has been viewed many times in sponsorship, particularly with luxury goods seeking to reach target markets through sport whose following have the right demographic background but also the passion for the sport and its athletes. The best examples are golf, F1, and tennis.

Case study 2.3 below, of luxury watchmaker Rolex sponsorship of the Australian Open, is one illustration.

Case study 2.3 Rolex and the Australian Open[3]

In 2017, the luxury Swiss watchmaker Rolex renewed its sponsorship deal with Australian Open (tennis), extending their deal until 2027, the 20th anniversary of the partnership. Rolex will remain the official timekeeper of the Australian Open, and its watches and timepieces will continue to be seen around the Rod Laver Arena, Margaret Court Arena, and John Cain Arena, as well as on the Open's digital and broadcast platforms. While not the highest-contributing sponsor to the event, Rolex remains an associate sponsor and perhaps the most well-known. The awareness of Rolex as a key sponsor of the event may also be due, in part, to Rolex's sponsorship of high-performing tennis players such as Roger Federer and Caroline Wozniacki, both winners of the 2018 Australian Open (and pictured wearing Rolex watches on their wrists while hoisting the trophy). Awareness levels around this deal may also be elevated due to the placement of the Australian Open as the first Grand Slam tournament of the calendar year.

As of 2019, Rolex also sponsors the other two Grand Slam tennis tournaments, the US Open and Wimbledon. With over 40 years of sponsoring premier tennis events, these Grand Slam sponsorships highlight Rolex's "long-term commitment to supporting the pinnacle of tennis" (in the words of Stewart Wicht, president and CEO of Rolex Watch USA). Rolex also continues to align itself with a long list of championship tennis players from across the globe, furthering its global reach toward viewers of the sport.

The fourth point from Copeland et al. (1996) is that sport sponsorship is a flexible channel, leveraging opportunities such as merchandising, cross-promotions, and dealer incentives that can be exploited. They were certainly well ahead of their time on this one, as recent evaluations in sport, including esports, fantasy sport, and sport betting, are illustrative of the multiplatform reach of sport, and the resulting possibilities for sponsors.

The sport sponsorship deal

A sport sponsorship deal, at a very basic level, is an agreement entered into between brand and a sport property. The brand, as sponsor, provides financial or nonfinancial support to a sport property, expecting to achieve certain objectives (awareness, changing perceptions, image transfer, increased sales, enhanced brand equity, etc.) as a return for that investment.

In any sponsorship deal, the media assets included play a significant role. Indeed, without the media, the sport industry would not be the leading area of sport sponsorship. For example, without the extensive media generated by the Olympic Games (television, print, social, digital, etc.), there would not be Olympic sponsors investing hundreds of millions of dollars in the Games. The media helps the Games reach literally billions of people – exponentially more than those going to the Olympic stadiums and attending in person. For the Tokyo Games, held in the summer of 2021 with limited fans on-site due to the pandemic, extensive media reach still allowed the Games to take place. The opening ceremonies of any Olympic Games are perhaps the best testimony to the power of the media, as approximately one hundred thousand fans attend the opening ceremonies in person, while reports (although they vary) suggest that about a billion people watch around the world via television.

Figure 2.1 outlines what is included in a typical sponsorship deal.

THE SPORT SPONSORSHIP DEAL

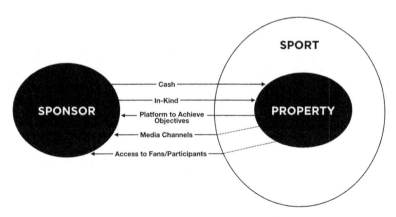

Figure 2.1 The Sport Sponsorship Deal.

Sport sponsorship is a three-way relationship between a brand, a property, and consumers. It is about placing a sponsor in an emotional relationship between a consumer (e.g., a soccer fan) and a sponsored activity (e.g., a soccer match involving a soccer team). Sponsors invest in the property to connect to consumers through the passion or interest they have, and to develop this passion into a sponsored asset to achieve their objectives. Unlike in philanthropic giving, a brand demands a return on its sponsorship investment. Sometimes, there are also agencies involved, representing either the brand or the property, to aid in the sponsor's ability to reach those consumers through the sport property.

As outlined in Figure 2.1, sport sponsorship is an exchange agreement between two parties in which resources are exchanged, and the exchange is weighed between what will be gained by each party and at what cost. Sponsors aim to achieve a variety of objectives in return for their sponsorship investment, with these objectives perhaps being the most important aspect for all parties involved. Both the sponsor (for business reasons) and the sport property (for renewal reasons) are interested in this exchange, particularly with the increasing investment in sponsorship (see Chapter 1) and the growing internal accountability facing sponsorship decision makers. This means that clearly defined sponsorship objectives need to be developed and formalized between sponsor and sport property. The remainder of this chapter looks at corporate objectives of sponsors, followed by stakeholders, proposals, and packages, all to inform about how to enter into and structure a sponsorship for success in achieving its objectives.

Corporate sponsorship objectives

Sponsorship is a promotional tool that can deliver many valuable and versatile benefits to a brand. It is rare for sponsors to set only a single objective in a sponsorship deal, since sponsorship by nature allows for the achievement of a number of objectives simultaneously. A study of many sponsorships found more than 150 different objectives that sponsors seek (O'Reilly & Madill, 2009). Further, different companies (brands) may have specific, predetermined types of goals they want to achieve from their sponsorship investment.

So, what are the different types of sponsorship objectives sought by sponsors? Let us explain, based on the considerable amount of time we have spent on this topic over our careers.

To appreciate the range of sponsorship objectives that exist, one has to first consider a sponsor's target audience(s), due to the fact that there are many. Sponsors may target a range of audiences including employees, investors, shareholders, owners, board members, volunteers, federal government departments, local and regional authorities, trade associations, fans, participants, community members, and many more. The most common primary target audiences of a sponsor are customers, potential consumers, and the public at large (i.e., society). Internal stakeholder objectives sought by brands through sponsorship can include:

- Employee satisfaction, recruitment, and retention
- Retailers, dealers, and distributors incentives through hospitality and entertainment
- Advancing the personal agendas and interests of senior executives
- Building goodwill among decision makers
- Boosting stock prices for shareholders
- Building business and trade relationships through corporate hospitality

A sponsor, for example, may offer a VIP hospitality experience to key partners, employees, brokers, suppliers, distributors, retailers, customers, and potential clients. Hospitality is an experiential marketing approach available via sponsorship activation, through which a sponsor may use their official sponsor status to reward an invitee with, for instance, free entry to the London Marathon, an all-expenses-paid trip to the Tokyo Olympic Games, or a luxury suite ticket to a Real Madrid game. These offers may also involve meeting players or coaches, being granted accreditation to a venue and access to VIP-only areas, and more, as a means to further heighten the VIP experience. Some brands adopt hospitality as a way to reward high performers (e.g., the top salespeople get to watch an NBA game from a suite). Further, the sponsorship of a popular sports club, athlete, or event can create a sense of pride among employees, which engenders the feeling of "my company cares" and "I'm part of the corporate team." It further helps boost employee morale through the perceived association with the sponsored club, athlete, or event. In turn, this can also reduce employee turnover.

As noted, the largest primary target audiences of a sponsor are typically customers, potential customers, and the public at large. In reaching out to target audiences, a sponsor's message is conveyed, delivered, translated, and understood differently by different segments of the audience. Segments include new versus existing customers of a sponsor as well as avid versus bandwagon fans of a sponsored sport club. Each of these groups will react differently to any given sponsorship.

The relative importance of a given sponsorship objective varies from one sponsor to another. Even within a sponsor's organization, the target can vary from one sponsorship to the next (e.g., new versus existing product). For example, an established and popular brand may sponsor one sport property to generate awareness about its new product and then sponsor another to increase brand recognition of one of its existing products.

You might now be wondering how we possibly make sense of all these objectives and scenarios within the custom world that is sport sponsorship.

Clearly, brands find sport to be an attractive sponsorship property and they aim to achieve many objectives through those sponsorship, but how do we make sense of it from a property side (sponsorship sales) or as a reader seeking to learn more about sponsorship objectives? In order to make this easier to understand and the facilitate practice, we have organized the many objectives and desired outcomes of a sponsorship deal into four different but interlinked sequential stages, as noted in Figure 2.2.

The four categories/stages noted in Figure 2.2 are awareness, understanding, liking, and reciprocity (sales). Each stage flows from the other stage prior. For instance, you cannot build a certain knowledge

CATEGORIES OF
SPONSOR OBJECTIVES

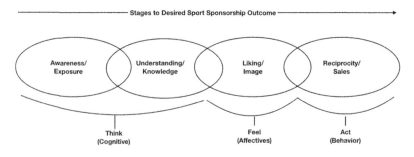

Figure 2.2 Categories of Sponsorship Objectives.

about a given product without first being exposed to it and being aware of it. Similarly, a sale will not happen unless there is some level of affect. Each of the four stages is discussed in the following paragraphs. The awareness stage is the (potential) consumer's initial point of exposure to a sponsor while the consumer is involved with the sport property. For a sponsorship to be effective, consumers have to recall the involvement of the brand in their experience. Then, if an individual is aware of a sponsor's involvement, they will be in a position to recall a sponsor, which leads to the understanding or knowledge stage, which typically involves message from the sponsor to inform about a product, or differentiate it from competitive offerings or to highlight the association with the sport property. If implemented effectively, the next phase would be about forming an attachment, leading ideally to a preference for the brand or a transfer of images associated with the sport property to the brand by the (potential) consumer. This, in turn, sets the stage for an intention to purchase the sponsor's product(s) and ideally, leading to the consumer buying the sponsor's offerings rather than those of its competitors.

Awareness/Exposure is an early-stage sponsor objective. Here, the brand seeks to create an initial exposure and recognition to a sponsored product, brand, or company, while the audiences are engaged with the sport property. Awareness can be sought using a number of different tactics, including on-site signage (banners, billboards), print outlets (newspaper coverage, posters, fliers), electronic channels (radio and TV coverage, as well as text marketing), and online platforms (social media and websites, email marketing). A logo placement or other creative approaches can be used to promote the partnership and make consumers of a sport property start to think about a sponsor's association to the property. A few examples of objectives related to awareness that sponsors aim to achieve include:

- Generating and increasing awareness of a product, a brand or a company
- Increasing media exposure
- Generating media benefits
- Increasing brand recognition
- Enhancing public awareness
- Reaching a new target market

An example of a brand (Liqui Moly) seeking awareness in the European marketplace is provided in the following case study.

Case study 2.4 Liqui Moly and Drift Masters European Championship (DMEC)[4]

The German-based automotive oil Liqui Moly and DMEC (Europe's professional drift series) announced a partnership for the 2020 season, a six-round series of small, custom-built auto-race circuits. Recognized as one of the world's best automotive additives, Liqui Moly made an excellent partner for the drift racing series. From various partnerships with auto-racing leagues, Liqui Moly looked to expand their brand awareness on the global stage, and create a win-win scenario for motorsports teams when they use Liqui Moly products. The company also signed a three-year deal with Formula 1, making them the official sponsor until the end of 2022 and furthering their reach and brand awareness into the automotive and auto-racing markets.

For DMEC and other auto-racing leagues, the partnership is not only about the road-going products produced by the German automotive oil company. In addition to the day-to-day products, Liqui Moly is a manufacturer of products meant to withstand the most demanding usage, ideal for auto racing. Furthermore, Liqui Moly's laboratories constantly update and evaluate their products based on the latest and greatest science and technology, providing their partners with ever better products, thus producing a better racing product for the auto-racing leagues.

Understanding/Knowledge is the stage at which consumers form a recollection of a sponsor and its business offerings, as well as acquire understanding about the sponsorship. For a sponsorship to be effective, consumers have to recall the sponsor's involvement, which requires activation. And without effective activation at this stage of the sponsorship process, it is daunting to achieve the subsequent, and more important, objectives of understanding/knowledge, liking/image, and sales/reciprocity. In seeking knowledge objectives, sponsors can put in place activation programs that educate key audiences about a product or brand in various ways, such as test services or product sampling. Rakuten's sponsorship of the Golden State Warriors NBA basketball team and FC Barcelona of La Liga are two good examples of a company adopting sponsorship to, first, create awareness about their offering, and then shift to educate audiences about its services, points of differences, and sales offers through activation, such as digital devices and TV commercials. A sample of some of the objectives sought by sponsors at the knowledge/understanding stage include:

- Informing potential customers about product and service features
- Showcasing unique (i.e., differentiated) product and service features
- Providing service and product sampling opportunities
- Rewarding existing customers
- Orienting benefits of offerings versus competitive products and/or services

Liking/Image is when the sponsor's target market perceives that the support the sponsor is providing to the sport property is a good deed (i.e., positive outcomes for the sport property and/or society at large). In an ideal situation, sponsors want the fans/followers/participants of a particular sport property to be associating and/or transferring positive feelings/images about the sport property to their brands.

Thus, many corporate sponsors seek to enhance or change their brand image by associating with a sport property. Liking/image is therefore a stage at which consumers start appreciating the support a sponsor is extending to the sport property that they have some attachment to (favorite team, admired athlete, national team, local team on a championship run, etc.). In turn, they form an emotional connection with the sponsor, which allows for activation to drive consumers to transfer the impressions, credibility, images, value, and passion they have associated with the sport to the sponsor. In cases, where an individual already possesses these attributes, the objective may be to alter or reinforce the image of a product, brand, or company. The case study that follows, Procter & Gamble's (P&G's) sponsorship of the National Women's Soccer League (NWSL), includes objectives at both the knowledge (e.g., sampling opportunities) and liking/image (e.g., public perception, goodwill, brand image) stages of the sponsor's desired sport sponsorship outcome.

Case study 2.5 Procter & Gamble/Secret deodorant and the National Women's Soccer League[5]

P&G and the NWSL have developed a history working together. In 2019, P&G's Secret deodorant brand spent $200,000 to purchase 9,000 NWSL game tickets "as part of the brand's growing effort to support equal pay and opportunity for women's soccer players." With 1,000 tickets purchased in nine NWSL cities, P&G distributed these tickets to local partners of the Secret brand, women's organizations, youth sports teams, and nonprofits. Additionally, P&G provided promotional giveaways such as Secret deodorant products, T-shirts, and spirit towels to the first 1,000 fans at each sponsored game. With Secret's brand recognized within the world of women's health, this partnership proved an ideal fit to provide support, recognition, and representation for female athletes: "This kind of support from Secret not only helps to fill seats for this one game, but it also sends a message to our broader community that we're here and we're worth watching" (in the words of Jessica McDonald, forward for North Carolina Courage NWSL team).

In 2020, this partnership continued in the form of P&G and Secret's sponsorship of the 2020 NWSL Challenge Cup, the return of the nine clubs to action following the COVID-19 hiatus. Hosted at Zions Bank Stadium in Herriman, Utah, an "athletes village" was set up for housing, training, and competition, and the Secret logo was plastered throughout. With athlete's social media presence and the Secret logo everywhere in sight, the deodorant brand received "pretty nuts ROI by getting in players' social media posts without even paying them directly."

P&G also donated USD$529,000 in 2019 to the labor union which represents the US Women's National Soccer team, furthering its relationship with women's soccer in America and stepping up on equal pay for women.

This ability of sponsorship to create liking and transfer images is particularly valuable in today's crowded marketplace, where sponsorship can help a brand stands out of the clutter and separate itself from their competitors and gain competitive advantage among its target audience that it reaches via its sport property partner. In certain cases, a sponsor may have the objective to be viewed as a good corporate citizen via a contribution to causes or local events, which can play a role in influencing consumer perceptions and attitudes. An often-cited example is British Petroleum's community events sponsorship program put in place following a 2010 oil spill.

Some of the objectives related to liking/image that sponsors aim to achieve include:

- Improving or changing public perceptions
- Transferring a particular image inherent to the sport property to the sponsor
- Attaining positive publicity (i.e., be seen as helping a property)
- Shaping consumer attitudes toward the sponsor
- Building goodwill toward the sponsor
- Maintaining, altering, or enhancing the sponsor's brand image
- Showcasing the sponsor's community support
- Cutting through advertising clutter
- Improving relationships with existing customers

Reciprocity/Sales. The most sought-after objective of any sponsor is increasing sales through reciprocity. Importantly, each of the first three stages (awareness/exposure, understanding/knowledge, and liking/image) is directly or indirectly related to increasing sales. In fact, we recommend that you view it as a continuum toward sales.

Increased sales from sponsorship can be achieved through both the short- and long-term impacts of the association through the activations that the sponsor implements. Short-term sales impacts are normally based on the sponsor objective to boost sales by selling its services and products at the venue attended by the target consumers. On the other hand, long-term sales impacts result from the objective for a sponsor to emotionally connect with consumers via the association with the sport property, which may lead to reciprocity (and sales), which means that passionate fans of the property will tend to buy services and products from a sponsoring company rather than a direct competitor.

Reciprocity/sales is an action stage at which fans/consumers/participants of a sport property appreciate the sponsor's involvement and build and intention to purchase the sponsor's offerings over those sold by competing brands. For example, it is common for a sponsor to receive media exposure as part of the sponsorship, which, in turn, can be used to communicate content that can lead to reciprocity/sales.

From the property side, the key to the reciprocity/sales stage is to be able to demonstrate to the sponsor that the sponsorship is helping them achieve sales outcomes. An important point here is that it is well known to be difficult to measure and attribute the role of the sponsorship in achieving sales outcomes to the specific sponsorship.

For instance, although it is possible to express an awareness objective by indicating that a certain number of people attended or watched or streamed an activation, it is much more difficult to determine the impact of that activation on the purchase behaviors of those same people. In the first three stages, the reporting is normally about what the sponsorship has produced (number of people reached, survey responses to associations, etc.).

Some of the objectives related to reciprocity/sales that sponsors aim to achieve include:

- Driving sales off site
- Boosting retail sales at a venue serving as a point-of-sale merchandising
- Growing the volume of product orders at the venue
- Increasing market share
- Reaching small segments and niches or target demographics, leading to sales or intent-to-purchase
- Gaining access to and sales in new markets and/or market segments
- Achieving (internal) sales objectives
- Growing sales volume and frequency with existing customers
- Increasing intent-to-purchase (note: this is often measured via the survey response of a potential customer of their desire to purchase the sponsor's product or service in the future as a result of the sponsorship).

The case study below provides some reporting on the sponsor's (Rwanda Development Board) objectives related to reciprocity and sales in a global sponsorship context.

Case study 2.6 Rwanda and Arsenal, PSG[6]

In 2018, the Rwandan Development Board signed a three-year, USD$39 million sleeve sponsoring deal with Arsenal FC, surprising the sponsorship world. Rwanda is listed as the 19th poorest country in the world with a per capita income of around USD$700, whereas Arsenal is one of the richest football clubs in the world. Given that Rwanda receives approximately USD$1.22 billion in financial aid from other nations, it is no surprise that some of these countries are not happy about Rwanda's investment in a football club.

For Rwanda, the deal is part of a larger tourism strategy. With numerous natural assets in their landscape and ecosystem, there are many reasons people may choose to visit Rwanda, especially with their further investment in RwandAir and high-end hotels. However, critics of the deal cite the Human Rights Watch's issuing of concerning reports about human rights abuse in the country as a risk for Arsenal.

However, after the first year of the deal, Rwandan officials cited an 8% increase in tourism numbers, with a 5% increase in tourists from the UK. Since the deal with Arsenal, Rwanda has doubled down on high-profile European football clubs to promote tourism, signing a three-year, approximately USD$13 million sponsorship deal with Paris-Saint Germain (PSG). The deal includes branding on warm-up jerseys worn by players prior to every match, and perimeter board signage around their home stadium. Visit Rwanda, Rwanda's tourism brand, also received player access rights for promotional work, including visits to the country. Furthermore, a PSG academy is set to be built in the nation's capital, Kigali. Reportedly, PSG approached Rwanda about setting up the deal after seeing the impact of the Arsenal deal.

More than boosting tourism and attracting investment, one can also argue that Rwanda is brilliantly using its sponsorship to repair the country's war-torn image (because of its civil war), which is referred to as soft power sponsorship. The sponsorship helps Rwanda improve its reputation, encourage reconciliation, gain trust in peace and security, and promote itself as a growing modern African nation.

Sponsorship stakeholders

In sponsorship, as noted, there are three key stakeholder groups, namely, sponsors, properties, and agencies.

Sponsors are the entities that seek to associate with a particular sport property to further their own marketing objectives. Sponsors may range from local coffee shop owners to multinational Fortune 500 corporations. These organizations become involved in sponsorship for a variety of reasons, seeking hundreds of objectives that we grouped into four stages above, from awareness/exposure to reciprocity/sales.

Sponsors are typically organized by the different industry categories in which they operate, where each category includes a group of similar companies that market similar products, at a similar price point, and to the same customers. Essentially, the members of each sponsorship category are direct competitors operating in the same industry category with market commonality.

Table 2.1 provides a list of industry categories, including some of the most common sponsors of sport properties. The table includes many of the industry categories that have an interest in sport properties, such as sporting goods, airlines, soft drinks and energy drinks, credit cards, beer, consumer goods, telecom, courier companies, automotive, electronics, banks, tires, insurance, hotels, fast food, transport companies, and security companies.

Sport properties, sometimes called sponsees, are the entities that receive rights fees from the sponsors in return for the marketing value they provide back. A sport property is, sometimes, referred to as a property owner or a rights holder (FIFA World Cup, Olympic Games, Real Madrid soccer club, Emirates Stadium, Virgin Money London marathon, local 5K run, city tennis championships tournament, etc.).

Determining the scope and reach of a property (i.e., the value it can provide) is one of the first considerations for sponsors seeking to identify sponsorships to invest in. Schwarz and Hunter (2018) categorize

Table 2.1 Categories and Brands in Sport Sponsorship

Sporting goods (e.g., Nike, Adidas, Puma)	Airlines (e.g., Emirates, Air Canada, Virgin)
Soft drink and energy drink (e.g., Coca-Cola, Pepsi)	Credit card (e.g., VISA, Mastercard)
Beer (e.g., Anheuser-Busch, Budweiser, Heineken)	Consumer goods (e.g., Procter & Gamble)
Telecom (e.g., T-Mobile, AT&T, Verizon)	Courier companies (e.g., UPS, FedEx, DHL)
Automotive (e.g., Toyota, Ford, Subaru)	Electronics (e.g., Omega, SONY, Samsung)
Banks (e.g., HSBC, Barclays, Scotiabank)	Tire (e.g., Bridgestone, Goodyear, Continental)
Insurance (e.g., Allstate, State Farm, GEICO)	Hotels (local)
Fast food (e.g., Burger King, McDonald's)	Security companies (e.g., G4S, JMG, Vector)
Transport companies (local)	Printing and publishing (local)

sport properties into seven groups. We have added an additional two categories (leagues and digital sport properties). Each is discussed briefly below and captured in Figure. 2.3 that follows the descriptions.

1   Governing body sponsorship: governing bodies are sport organizations that are responsible for the governance of sport at a local, regional, national, continental, or international level. Examples include the International Olympic Committee (IOC), Fédération Internationale de Football Association (FIFA), and the National Collegiate Athletic Association (NCAA). For example, the Olympic Games attract multinational sponsors, including Coca-Cola and Samsung.

2   League sponsorship: leagues are the entities responsible for a professional sport in a given jurisdiction. Examples include the NFL, the English Premier League (EPL), and the Indian Premier League (IPL). The IPL, for instance, has had a title sponsor since its inception and is currently the VIVO IPL, with past title sponsors including DLF and Pepsi. The case study below provides further details.

Case study 2.7 Dream11 and the Indian Premier League in 2020[7]

From its launch in 2008 up to 2022, the Indian Premier League has featured four different title sponsors, DFL (2008–2012), Pepsi (2013–2015), VIVO (2016–2017 and 2018–2019), Dream11 (2020), and VIVO again (2021 to 2022). Within the history of the league, two title sponsors have terminated their contract prior to its agreed time. Pepsi signed a five-year deal in 2013, and pulled out just prior to a corruption scandal around the 2015 championship tournament. VIVO, the Chinese mobile manufacturing giant, after signing a five-year renewal deal terminated the contract early following the armed conflicts between China and India which led to anti-China sentiments across India. After VIVO's exit, the board of the IPL was happy to land Dream11 as a title sponsor, albeit at half the value of the VIVO deal, for the 2020 season. VIVO then returned as title sponsor for the 2021 and 2022 seasons. The Dream11 scenario provides an example of the risks associated with sponsorship naming rights for a given sports league, as sponsors can quickly change their stance and terminate contracts, based on things out of the control of the sport property itself, such as political issues between countries. In 2019, via a four-year deal, Dream11 actually came on board as an official sponsor (a lower and less expensive level than being title sponsor) of the IPL prior to VIVO's stepping out in 2020. Additionally, the "Official Fantasy Game" of IPL is powered by Dream11, a fantasy sports organization. Dream11 provides millions of fans with a platform to create their fantasy cricket teams, and features in-depth data about players and teams on their website, in addition to marketing cricket as their premier sport on landing pages. The IPL targeted Dream11 as an official sponsor, recognizing their upwards trending online viewership numbers and the popularity of the IPL among fantasy sports fans in India. According to the 2019 IFSG-KPMG report, fantasy cricket is the most widely played online fantasy sports game in the world.

3   Team/Club sponsorship: sports teams exist at many different levels, namely, high school, college, local, professional, and national. For relatively small sport sponsorships, such as a local call dealer sponsoring a local high school team, the sponsor can achieve their objectives.

4   Athlete sponsorship: athlete sponsorship refers to companies that sponsor athletes at any level, from professional to youth. This is sometimes called, even though not entirely the same, athlete endorsement, where it is positioned that the athlete endorses the brand's products or services in return for cash or in kind sponsorship. For example, Nike is well known for sponsoring a number of track and field athletes financially as well as providing kits (i.e., equipment packages of apparel, shoes, and other gear), such as Kenyan runner Eliud Kipchoge.

5   Sport media channel sponsorship: this property type refers to companies that purchase programming for sport-related broadcast and streaming on different television, radio, and digital channels. The broadcast programs are commonly sponsored. For example, in the United States, American Express sponsors the half-time show of a regular-season NBA broadcast on TNT.

6   Facility sponsorship: facility sponsorship refers to sponsorship of a venue (stadium, arena, training center, etc.), either as title

sponsor or sponsor of a portion of the venue (e.g., naming of a pool or an entrance or a lounge area within a venue). The most important facility sponsorship is the "naming rights" scenario where the sponsor is the title sponsor of the venue, meaning that the venue is named after the sponsor for a defined period of time. Naming rights typically range from 3 to 30 years in length and are common in multipurpose arenas, performing arts venues, arenas, and stadiums. In the United States, most (about 85%) of the teams in the major four professional sport leagues play in named venues. A key point is that even though the venues are named, the sponsoring companies do not own the stadiums but only the naming rights. An example is Canadian bank Scotiabank's recent deal with the Downtown Toronto arena that is home to the Toronto Raptors of the NBA and the Toronto Maple Leafs of the NHL. The bank signed a reported 20-year CND$800 million agreement to rename Air Canada Centre as Scotiabank Arena in 2017.

7   Event sponsorship: sport events range from small local events (e.g., local golf tournament) to global mega events (e.g., Tour de France, Confederation of African Football Champions League). There are many more events in sport than available sponsors in different parts of the world, so sponsorship for smaller events is challenging to find. An example of an event sponsorship is the New York Marathon, who signed an eight-year contract with Tata Consultancy Services (TCS) in 2013 to name the event after the sponsor, TCS New York Marathon.

8   Sport-specific sponsorship: This type of sponsorship involves a brand partnering with a sport property in order to reach a specific niche market. The portfolio of sponsorships by the energy drink manufacturer Red Bull is an example of trying to read the market of adventure sport participants, Ironman triathletes, and ultramarathoners.

9   Digital sport product sponsorship. A relatively new area of sport sponsorship is brands using the digital platforms of esports, fantasy sports, and online sport betting, to reach those consumers. Esport sponsors include brands like Intel, HyperX, and Sony.

A key point of both #8 and #9 above is that sport sponsorship enables companies to direct their sponsorship efforts through the platform provided by a particular sport, and, in turn, a specific target market of interest.

Agencies refer to the third-party firms who work for brands and/ or properties on sponsorship related work. Sometimes, these are ad

Figure 2.3 Categories of Sport Properties. Adapted from Schwarz and Hunter (2018).

agencies, sometimes marketing agencies, and more and more often, they are sponsorship agencies (i.e., agencies specialized in sponsorship). These agencies range from global entities with thousands of employees to single-person shops in any developed country of the world. Their roles vary considerably by agency, by sponsorship, and by client. In some cases, an agency will take on the role of "agency-of-record", or AOR, where they will take responsibility for much of the sponsorship function or a brand or a property. Sponsorship sales agencies, similarly, may take on the role of selling sponsorship for a property, including all categories and stages of the sales cycle. More often, however, agency work is done on a contract by contract basis, where the agency is hired to do a specific task (value a particular property, develop a sponsorship strategy, evaluate a sponsorship, develop the creative, implement an activation, etc.).

Agencies may be a new nuance of sponsorship for you, since, often, we are exposed to the official association formed between a sponsor and a sponsored party, and we assume that it is just those two parties who are directly involved in the sponsorship. However, in any sizeable sponsorship, there are normally agencies involved representing and working on behalf of both the sponsors and the property, taking on roles in developing, researching, proposing, negotiating, valuating, and implementing a sponsorship. They have the expertise, experience, resources, skilled people and rich networks to support their clients. Examples of agencies who operate in sponsorship at a global level include Wasserman, IEG, GMR, and Octagon.

The sponsorship proposal

The nine property areas of sport sponsorship investment illustrate sponsorship's ability to reach different markets through different sports and different sport properties. In most of sponsorships, both the sponsor and the property are challenged to defend and justify the investments made. Hence, a sponsor's decision on sponsorship spending require in-depth research that provides compelling reasons to justify an investment. Thus, to even get a sponsor to consider their property as a partner, a sport property must prepare a sponsorship proposal to submit for consideration to the brand. Such a proposal has to stand out from the (often hundreds of) competing proposals that the brand will consider.

So, how do you make sure that your proposal can actually stand out? Well, it is not easy and the following section is designed to provide guidance, by covering the planning steps and tasks involved in developing a proposal to demonstrate the promotional potential of a sport property.

AUTHORS' BLOG: WRITER'S CHAMP

There are few things as challenging as writing a sponsorship proposal.

That very menacing blank page is staring back at you and taunting you, and challenging you to make one false move.

You felt confident in your research, your due diligence, and your understanding of the sponsor prospect. You have confidence in your property's innate knowledge, and more so in the value that you believe it can bring to the partner. You have faith in knowing that you have written a thousand proposals before.

But this is not just #1001. This one is different. Why? Because they are all different. It is one of the frustrations of the sponsorship industry. Long before you entered this sector, perhaps before you were born, sponsorship practitioners realized that no two proposals could be alike. (Amazingly, it seems salespeople still boast with great pride that they customize every request, which is akin to a restaurant offering you tap water. Everybody customizes.)

Not only is this proposal #1001, but it feels like the most important proposal you have ever written. You want a deal with this partner. They are the partner that your boss wants you to land. Heck, even your head coach or tournament director has texted you about this company. You have tracked their social media sites, read about their other deals, and shared their marketing leads talk at conferences. You want this one so bad. So, why can't you take what you have written before and make it work? Because that last one was not this one. At this point, all the writing in this blog has done is to distract you from writing that darn proposal. You need help, and you need it now. So let's go. Let's look at five key secrets to writing a great pitch.

#1 Begin with the end in mind

You should thank Stephen Covey for the best writing advice ever. Start your proposal by writing the big finale. The crescendo. The ask. The bumper sticker. See below. If you are still stuck, write the Thank-You Page. If you still suck, write an outline, which we always advise. But when you write the outline, begin with the end. Consider the outcome you dream of, and work backwards from there. If the result is a chance for a meeting, write your proposal to get an appointment by describing how it will be the most critical meeting ever. If it is an opportunity to negotiate, convince them why they should. If the outcome is to get them to agree to the proposal, then visualize them making that decision and the reason for doing so.

#2 The CFO has a vote

You may not want to admit it, but even if your proposal does not have money or financial requests included, the recipients will make an ROI assessment. At some point, the CFO, the COO, and the CEO are going to ask the question. What are we getting out of this? How is it improving our community? Write your proposal to convince the CFO that your sponsorship will be money well spent.

#3 Write a movie script

Sponsorship proposals are not your last will, legal documents, or doctoral thesis. Are they ingredient lists or instructions for self-assembled furniture? Perhaps you perceive them to be akin to an owner's manual or a warranty. Think of your proposal as a script or canvas on which you connect with the reader. Like any great script, your pitch must tell a story. The story is more vital than the information because the emotional connection you are creating is between you and the buyer. You want that buyer to envision themselves and their brand as the heroine of the script—the one facing down long odds and triumphantly overcoming. If you have never read, written, or paid attention to the dialogue, now is the time.

#4 It is you, not me

This message is the opposite headline from the last time you got dumped, remember? *It is me, not you.* What a load of crap! But in writing a proposal, it is you, not me. So take the mental time to flip that sentiment around because sponsorship is genuinely about the sponsor. You need to audit your proposal for a share of voice. If you are not talking about your prospects on a 3:1 ratio, you are doomed. The buyer does not care about you. Not yet. But they will when you start demonstrating how much you care about them. It is time to rebound from that dumping and get into a full-court wooing.

#5 Write your bumper sticker

We know bumper stickers are getting outdated, so feel free to replace this with social profile, Tweet, or billboard. But we want to challenge you to get your entire proposal down to a bumper sticker. Can your pitch be summarized in five to seven words? If you don't know what a bumper sticker is, search for one online. Why do we want your pitch distilled so tightly? Because five to seven words are all that people will recall from your deck. Yes, it is true. Because five to seven are all, most people have time to utter in a hallway conversation or a quick chat with their boss. It is true. You want your entire pitch to be a memorable headline that every stakeholder can convey with conviction and passion.

Bonus tip: writing of all types is a difficult task. There are a standard set of recommendations for first-time authors:

- Write every single day
- Write at the same time every day
- Write for at least two hours uninterrupted

- Write in the same location
- Write freely without fear of error

All three of us have experience writing books and this approach helped us all significantly in writing our previous books. We recommend that you reserve a part of your day for writing your proposals. Each of us has different approaches to this and we recommend you do the same. Norm writes best from 10pm to 4am, Gashaw prefers 1pm to 5pm, while Mark's writing mind is best at work early in the morning or the last two hours before he sleeps.

Mark notes that there is an added benefit to writing late at night when he gets stumped. Often by merely thinking about the writing task and allowing it time to cycle through his brain as he sleeps, he ends up coming up with the aha moment the next day, his brain finding the pithy words, the red thread he has been hunting.

One piece of advice that many authors share, including us, to first-time writers is that you do not have to work on your book every day, but you do have to think about it.

This concept, thinking about your writing daily, has been a game-changing advice for all of us, whether it is for books, keynotes, webinars, case studies, conference presentations, papers, or client presentations.

Now, let us get to the task of providing you with insight into how to build a great proposal.

There are two different but interrelated steps that need to be completed in developing a winning sponsorship proposal. These tasks are (i) gathering input for the proposal and (ii) developing the proposal. The "gathering inputs" step includes four planning steps: preparing an inventory of offerings, identifying a target market, prospecting for a sponsor, and researching short-listed sponsors. In the "developing a sponsorship proposal" step, we outline ten different sections that need to be included in the document: cover page, property highlights, property description, property's market segment, property's audience reach, activation offers, benefits inventory, sponsorship fee, call for action, and cover letter.

Gathering input

Gathering inputs for a proposal is crucial for a successful sponsor hunt. It allows you to use your resources (time, human resources, money, knowledge, equipment, media assets, etc.) more efficiently and effectively. In gathering inputs about a potential sponsor, a sport property needs to undertake the following four planning steps: (i) preparing an inventory of offerings, (ii) identifying target markets, (iii) prospecting for a sponsor, and (iv) researching short-listed sponsors. Each of these steps is discussed below.

Inventory: The first step in developing a sponsorship proposal is to conduct an inventory of what one can offer in exchange for a sponsorship rights fee. Sometimes, these items are called "assets" and are part of an "asset profile" for the sport property. These can include things like events, athletes, brand, logos, fan bases, participant databases, and sanction rights to host a championship.

The task of building an inventory of assets starts with identifying pre-event, during-event, and postevent marketing communication efforts. This includes identifying any online (e.g., social media and web-based platforms), television, radio, print (e.g., newspapers, magazines), and outdoor (e.g., banner, posters, fliers, billboards) communication channels available to a potential sponsor via the sport property and its assets. On each of these channels, it is key to describe the media reach of your event before, during, and after the event, particularly in relation to live transmissions on high-volume channels like television, Facebook, and YouTube.

It is a brief profile of results from previous years in terms of media coverage (television ratings, social media hits, YouTube views, etc.), participation/spectator levels/engagement, the breakdown of attendees, demographics of viewers, benefits provided to sponsors, and any other result that would be potentially relevant to a future sponsor. Often, the inventory of assets provided in a proposal will include lists based on the following categories of assets: (i) on-site (e.g., space to carry out on-site experiential, hosting, and sampling opportunities), (ii) signage (e.g., on-site event, vehicle signage, logo on uniforms), (iii) digital (website banners, social media links, etc.), (iv) hosting (e.g., tickets to the event, VIP tickets, athlete or celebrity meet-and-greets), (v) database marketing (e.g., access to fan, spectator or participant contact information), and (vi) media opportunities (e.g., pre- and postevent press conference).

Listing all the available opportunities with your sport property does not mean that you are going to offer everything in your inventory to any company willing to pay for it. Doing so could overcommercialize and potentially impact the core product of your sport property. Yet, by including the inventory of assets in the proposal, it allows the potential sponsor to recognize the promotional potential of a sponsorship. Further, by having such an inventory in place, it can help establish pricing and different tiers of sponsorship. Clearly, a detailed and specific listing of all available opportunities for a sponsor is essential. A sample inventory for a small local 5K run is provided below.

SAMPLE SPONSORSHIP INVENTORY FROM A LOCAL 5K RUN

Unique offerings

Workshop

Opportunity for informational session about your services – as race participants arrive at registration centers to pick up their race bib, and public announcements on the race day.

Generate leads and sales
Using promo codes to drive sales where participants will be encouraged to try a sample and get 5% discount on race entry fee

Social media
Developing hashtags and promotional campaign messages and communicating and reaching out to the event followers
   Engagement opportunities, where selected race participants' testimony of your company in a 30-second video
   Arranging photo contest among participants about their best experience of your companies service to be promoted on all the event's promotional mediums including social media

General offerings

General
The title sponsors will receive extensive and prominent position, and placement on all publicity materials and on venue sites before, during, and after the events. Title sponsorship position offers the maximum exposure on all the three events.

Naming
Recognized as the official Title Sponsor of the event with event being named, "XYZ Company EVENT NAME 5K Run".
YOUR COMPANY name incorporated into event logo
Event name and logo on all marketing materials
Event named "XYZ Company EVENT NAME 5K Run" on all event listings and schedules
Opportunity for creative, customized, on-site promotions (This package can be customized to fit your company's marketing/promotion goals.)

Bib number
Title logo to appear on all participants' race bibs

Banners
Your company brand to receive maximum exposure on start/finish area
Start/Finish area: 4 banners in the start/finish area, and 4 flying banners"
On racecourse: 4 banners

Backdrop
Your logo or name will appear on the backdrop that will displayed at all awarding ceremonies. Your logo or name will appear on the backdrop that will displayed at all press conferences.

Public announcement
You will be acknowledged in public address announcements prior to, during and after the event.

Start and finish gantry
Your company logo will appear on the columns of the start and finish gantry.

Finish line tape
A title sponsor logo will be displayed on the finish line that will be crossed by top finishers.

Website
Your logo will appear on the official events website with a link to your official website.

Press conference
A press conference announcing a title sponsor will be organized soon after the signing of the sponsorship agreement. A press conference announcing sponsors of the event will be held ahead of the events.

Press releases
A media campaign (online, electronics, outdoor, and print) will be organized to announce your partnership with the event, and post-event release to thank sponsors for their support.

Print
Letter Heads: all correspondences made soon after the signing of the sponsorship agreement will bear the title logo.

Official Results: all official results given out to the media, officials, and delegates will bear the title logo.

Accreditation: all accreditations used by VIPS, guests, athletes, officials, and media will bear the title logo.

Info Pack: one-page information of your company will be inserted into participants' race pack.

Hospitality
Engage agents/Reach potential employees: your agents and branch office employees get opportunity to train for the race for four weekends run up to the event and designing your promotional campaigns for these four sessions.

Customization
This partnership package can be customized to fit your companies marketing objectives.

Others
Opportunity for creative and customized on-site promotions (at the event site) including a booth to distribute promotional materials

Opportunity for your company representative to present awards to winners of the event

Your company representatives will be invited to all associated events and postevent dinners.

Identifying the Target Audience: articulating your market segment and defining the attractiveness of your audience to a potential sponsor is key to both identifying potentially interested sponsors and, in turn, attracting and retaining a sponsor. As introduced at the begging of this chapter, in sponsorship, target market segmentation can be seen in terms of who your fans/customers are (demographics), why they care about the sport property (psychographics), where they are in relation to your property (geographic), and why they are interested in your property (benefits). With respect to benefits, these are often characterized as "uses and gratifications", where uses are the tangible things that a fan/participant gets out of their involvement (e.g., entertainment value, family experience) and gratifications are the feelings of pleasure, satisfaction, and emotion that the involvement leads to (e.g., the highs and lows of a diehard fan).

Specific to the proposal, it is recommended that a breakdown of the property's audience in terms of demography (e.g., gender, age, race, ethnicity, marital status), socioeconomic features (e.g., income, education, occupation), and geographic characteristics (e.g., local, regional, national, and global market segments) is shared, with as much detail as you have. The goal is to provide the potential sponsor with the details of who they can potentially reach with the sponsorship. The more data you have on your audience, the higher the selling power of your proposal.

Prospecting: once the inventory of assets is complete and the target market breakdown is prepared, the next step is to prospect for potential sponsors. In this context, prospecting refers to identifying a list of potential sponsors who might have interest in your assets and target markets. Specifically, this involves identifying a set of matching potential sponsors for your property. It is important to remember that this step is about staying efficient and avoid wasting resources pursuing brands who do not share your audience or value the assets you have.

Since sponsorship is an agreement between two parties whereby resources are exchanged, a sponsorship deal must be viewed as mutually beneficial by both sponsor and property, or it will never come to fruition. Thus, as a property, you need to identify a set of potential sponsors that would be interested in your target audience and inventory.

Thus, your inventory and target audience should guide you in identifying a list of potential sponsors. A recommended way to identify such a list starts by defining the reach of your sport property. Once you know your reach, you can narrow down the list of potential sponsors. In a simple example, a sport property with a local reach would not normally be of interest to a sponsor who seeks national and global coverage. In this example, a local grocery store would be a better target than a multinational company such as Procter & Gamble. The following three considerations are provided to guide a sport property in identifying a list of potential sponsors:

Table 2.2 Industry Categories of NASCAR Sponsors

Premier Partners

Official Beer

Official Fan Refreshment
Official Insurance Partner
Official Cable Service Provider, Official
  Series Sponsor
Series Entitlement Partners
Official Cable Service Provider, Official
  Series Sponsor
Official Outdoor Company, Official
  Series Sponsor
Official Partners of NASCAR

Official Partner (no category named)
Official Auto Parts Retailer
Official Cloud Partner

Official Emergency Medical Services
  Partner
Official Paint
An Authorized Gaming Partner of
  NASCAR
Official Pain Relief Cream
Official Vacation Ownership Provider
Official Beer
Official Fan Refreshment
Official Vodka
Official Daily Fantasy Sports Game

Official Trackside Retailer
Official Daily Fantasy Sports Game

Official RV & Outdoor Retailer
  of NASCAR
Official Roadside Assistance of
  NASCAR
Official Tire
Official Filter
Official Chocolate

Official Hauler
Official High-Performance Glove
  of NASCAR
Official Motor Oil

Official Energy Drink of
  NASCAR
Official Private Aviation Partner
Official Filter
Official Health Technology
  Partner
Official Grill

Official Bank
Official Antifreeze/Coolant

Official Luxury Motorcoach
Official Supplier
Official Moonshine
Official Satellite Radio Partner
Official Fuel
Official Telecommunications
  Partner
Official Vehicle Illumination Lights
Official NASCAR Green Partner
NASCAR Performance Partner

Source: Adapted from https://www.nascar.com/officialsponsors

i Limit to sponsors whose target market is similar to the sport property,
ii Consider the sponsors of other properties who are similar to yours, and
iii Expand to the direct industry competitors of the potential sponsors identified in (i) and (ii) above.

Table 2.2, which shares the list of NASCAR official partners from different industry categories, is provided as an example.

Researching Short-Listed Potential Sponsors: the next step in this process is to conduct research on each of the short-listed sponsors from the prior step. It is recommended that this research should address, among other factors, the following points.

*   *Assess whether there is a natural fit with the potential sponsor.* This means you should show that there is an overlap between your fan/ participant base and the sponsor's target market. Use segmentation factors to identify the target audience (family status/role, ethnicity, gender, living situation, etc.). For example, if your sport property is a private golf club, you would seek sponsors whose target markets match (golfers, middle to upper income, older age group, etc.).
*   *Gather information to gauge the potential sponsor's interest in your property.* Start gathering information online (e.g., industry reports, media coverage), and data can also be gathered from the potential sponsor's digital communication platforms (e.g., website, social media). Case study 2.8 below reports on a company (Unibet, an online sport betting service) that is sponsoring a major sport property showing high interest in amateur sport properties in France.

Case study 2.8 Unibet and France's amateur sport (and PSG)[8]

Unibet (an online sport betting service) and Paris Saint-Germain Football Club (PSG) extended the duration of their sponsorship deal until the end of the 2022–2023 season, with extended rights into new regions outside Europe, including the United States and Australia. The original deal, from 2018–2019 to 2019–2020, with European rights only, was believed to be worth $1.66 million per season. Unibet and PSG have activated numerous campaigns, including poster campaigns, television commercials (TVCs), and initiatives using the club's social media channels (which have more than 80 million fans globally). With a championship caliber team such as PSG, Unibet will have access to an extensive fan base with their extended partnership.

But what does this mean for amateur sport in France? In France, both lottery games and sports betting revenues directly contribute to the National Sports Agency (NSA) budget, which, in turn, subsidizes sports clubs at local levels. As of September 2020, only 15% of the Sports tax on betting went toward funding the NSA, while the rest went toward the State budget. However, some members of the French Parliament suggested increasing the share which funds local sports. Unibet activated #AuCoeurDuFootball (#AtTheHeartOfFootball) in 2018, enabling them to equip 235 local French clubs and 11,200 players in football kits over two years. In the second season of the partnership, over 6,000 clubs applied on the Unibet platform, demonstrating the huge potential of national sponsors to reach and support local teams and exemplifying Unibet's motto of "By Players, For Players".

Additionally, Parions Sport, Française des Jeux's sports betting brand, announced their sponsorship of 100 amateur football clubs throughout France in 2020, furthering the connection between sports betting and local sports clubs in France.

- *Investigate the financial ability of the potential sponsor.* Although this could be a difficult task, it is important to assess the ability of the potential sponsor to provide the resources that the proposal will ask of them. A number of public sources (annual reports, stock exchanges, media releases) and industry publications (e.g., country economic monitors) may provide what is needed. The point here is to eliminate any potential sponsors who would not be able to provide what you need. At this point, you will have narrowed down your list and have a clear idea about which potential sponsors remain who might consider your proposal.
- *Prioritize your list.* Classify your list based on your assessment of the likelihood that they will agree to your proposal. If your list is long, you can consider prioritizing with groups of potential sponsors by category (banking, retail, etc.).

- *Determine the needs of each of your short-listed potential sponsors.* This is a key step in the proposal process. Based on your research from earlier steps, your industry network, industry level data from government sources (e.g., census data, sector reports), and secondary online search, a needs assessment of each potential sponsor is undertaken. Potential needs that you might identify include a potential sponsor's interest in introducing a new product, creating awareness of an underperforming service, building a positive image in a community following a crisis, and building business and trade relationships with local government to drive global expansion. As part of this needs assessment, it is essential to identify unique promotional opportunities available via your property that are fitting and appealing to each potential sponsor on your highest-priority list.
- *Identify the right contact.* Determine who is the correct person to connect with. This is typically the decision maker on sponsorship for the potential sponsor.

Developing the sponsorship proposal

On completion of the "gathering input" stage, the next step involves actually putting together the proposal for those sponsors on your short list. This should result in a document that is able to communicate your property benefits to a potential sponsor in a clear, logical, and meaningful way. Crafting a proposal requires careful handling of the research from the gathering input steps.

Although you do need to present the scope, size, and magnitude of your property, a proposal is not about the size of your property, but rather about the benefits that you can/will provide to the potential sponsor. Demonstrating the fit and uniqueness of your property to the sponsor is what matters. To do so, you should be able to tell a meaningful and appealing story specific to that potential sponsor (i.e., each proposal should be adapted to the recipient). Although there are many models out there and formats to consider, we suggest that your proposal have ten different sections/content pieces.

1 *Cover page*: the cover page should have a descriptive picture of your event or a quote about your property from a credible source (e.g., a testimony from a participant or past sponsor).
2 *Property highlights*: this is a short (preferably one page or one slide in a deck format) section that provides an overview of your property, including your scale, reach, scope, date, key assets, past

achievements, and how often your events will be happening (i.e., a season-long set of games like the English Premier League, an annual event like the Berlin Marathon, a one-off music concert, or a 20-year stadium naming of a venue). The goal of this section is to incentivize the reader to read on. Thus, you need to highlight the value of your property to your consumers in this section and extend that value to what it could bring to the potential sponsor who you are writing for. Always remember that sponsorship is about establishing emotional connection between a sponsor and your audience through your property.

3 *Property description*: this section (could be an additional page or one or two slides) should be brief and descriptive and cover the basics of your property. For example, if your property is a sport event, you need to inform the sponsor of the nature of the event, its location and venue, the event date, and a very brief description of attendees (e.g., celebrities, if any).

4 *Property market segments*: in this section, a page/slide or two in length, we recommend that you provide content to help the potential sponsor answer the question, "Who do I reach?" Here, you need to offer demographic, psychographic, and geographic data about your target audience to show your property's fit and compatibility with the sponsor. You should also provide data on benefits sought and socioeconomic features of your audience. You may not need to provide information on all these data points; focus on those that help show compatibility between the potential sponsor and consumers your event can reach.

5 *Property audience reach*: in this section, a page/slide or two in length, you answer the question, "What would be the size of my sponsorship footprint?" Accordingly, you need to provide information about the audience you will be reaching and the mediums you would use to accomplish that; these include your efforts before, during, and after the marketing communication efforts. The communication mediums may include online (e.g., social media with the number of followers, email marketing, and web-based platforms), electronics (e.g., text messages, marketing, TV, radio), print (e.g., newspapers, magazines), and outdoors (e.g., posters, fliers, billboards). Any live transmissions you intend to have on TV, Facebook, and YouTube should be presented. You can support this with previous success stories in terms of media coverage, participant level, and celebrity attendance.

6 *Activation offers*: in this section, a page/slide or two in length, you help a potential sponsor answer the question, "How best can I use this sponsorship?" Accordingly, you need to propose, at least, four to eight creative ideas that describe how the potential sponsor can achieve what your research (discussed earlier in the prospecting section) found to be their intended objectives, whether creating awareness, branding, educating customers, image transferring, inducing sales, and so on. In this section, you need to clearly demonstrate how you would link your target market to the unique promotional opportunities you have developed for the given sponsor. Opportunities for the sponsor to do sampling, speaking, database marketing, sales promotions, and other activations should be highlighted. Two examples are (i) a sales promotion of "If you use the sponsor's product/service, you will get a 50% discount" or (ii) a 30-second video of two players' positive testimony of your service/product.

7 *Benefits inventory*: in this section, a page/slide or two in length and based on the prework done (as noted earlier), you should list the benefits that are available via an association with your sport property. These benefits may include banners at the venue, a short video clip on the venue's video board, logos on tickets, logos on T-shirts, free tickets to employees, social media assets, and television commercials. The box provided earlier about the 5K run has a useful list to build from.

8 *Sponsorship fee*: in this section, a page/slide in length, we recommend that you do not provide a predetermined (exact) dollar figure. We recommend this due to the fact that sponsorship commitments can vary depending on such factors as level of sponsorship (title, presenting, associate, supporting), length of the commitment (one-off, multiple years), exclusivity, level of their readiness to commit resources, the timeliness required to aid the sponsor in achieving their objectives, and the breakdown of cash versus value-in-kind (VIK) (e.g., hotel rooms, air tickets, bottled water). Further by attaching a sponsorship fee that is viewed to be too high by the potential sponsor, it can lead to the sponsor losing interest. If you can get their interest without sharing a fee, it can (ideally) lead to a meeting where you can discuss the document further in an in-person meeting where you can customize your offer. Of course, you need to know your sought price (or range) before you go into those meetings, but we suggest that you wait as long as possible before disclosing.

9 *Call to action*: since the purpose of a proposal is to get an invite to further discuss your offer, we recommend that you end by stating that the package is open for customization. This should include a "call to action" where you share your contact information, invite them to reach out for a follow-up, and ask the prospective sponsor to provide their input and offer them to modify the proposal to suit their needs. Be very clear that you are flexible to have open discussions and share your availability.

10 *Cover letter:* this is a suggested piece that accompanies the pro-posal, but is not necessarily part of it. Yes, although a cover letter is not considered one of the core sections of a sponsorship proposal, it is an integral part of a proposal. Whether a formal document or a cover email, it accompanies your proposal by introducing your property and business offer to a potential sponsor. It should be crafted in a way (concise and precise) that encourages the sponsor interested in reading the whole proposal. Thus, it should have con-tent specific to the potential sponsor with some of your key selling points highlighted in a succinct way.

Figure 2.4 summarizes our process for a sponsorship proposal.

BUILDING A SPONSORSHIP PROPOSAL

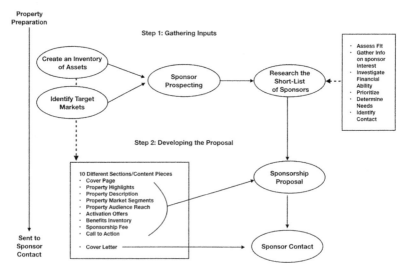

Figure 2.4 Sponsorship Proposal.

Postsponsorship proposal

If, as the sport property, you are invited to discuss the proposal further in a meeting, you will need to prepare your presentation. In this scenario, the deck (i.e., PowerPoint, Keynote, Google Slides, etc.) version is recommended, often accompanied by digital enhancements such as a video clip, photos, links, and updated content that adds to the original proposal. Digital and (if appropriate) hard copies should be prepared and presented to all of those attending the presentation. These presentations or pitches are usually organized so that your presentation is followed by a question-and-answer session. We advise to be very attentive to the questions and use the opportunity to understand the sponsor's needs and concerns, as the next step – if a decision to accept or reject your proposal is not made – might be to revise your proposal.

On receiving the outcome of the potential sponsor's decision, regardless of the outcome, stay professional. In the case of a negative response, thank the sponsor for inviting you to make a proposal, and use the opportunity to establish positive relations for any future possibilities. In the case of positive news, be prepared to answer questions related to any aspect of your proposal and be ready for negotiations around price, assets to be included, access to databases, and athletes. Be ready with pricing information related to the level of the sponsorship (i.e., title, presenting, associate, etc.) or any of the assets included in your proposal (inventory).

Sponsorship packages

If you are successful in coming to an agreement with a sponsor, a contract will be signed that will include an agreed-to sponsorship package. A sponsorship package includes all of the elements of the sponsorship that you, the property, agree to provide and all the deliverables or commitments that the sponsor expects from you. Sponsorship packages are a reflection of the sponsorship agreement, and really are the most customized aspect of the sponsorship contract. A sponsorship package can also be described as the agreed-on approach to the activation and servicing of the sponsorship that the two parties settle on to execute together.

Some of the most common elements included in a sponsorship package are exclusivity, right to use event trademarks and logos, sponsorship level, placement of signage, distribution rights, link on the event website, social media cross-promotion, and hospitality offerings. Each of these elements will be discussed in further detail in Chapter 4.

Notes

1 https://www.reuters.com/article/esports-lol-top-esports/top-esports-land-beats-by-dre-as-sponsor-idUSFLM8B0M06; https://esportsinsider.com/2020/10/top-esports-beats-electronics-sponsorship/; https://esportsinsider.com/2020/12/beats-by-dr-dre-reveals-special-edition-faze-clan-branded-headphone/

2 https://www.sportbusiness.com/news/mtn-seeks-to-extend-headline-springboks-sponsorship/#:~:text=South%20African%20telecoms%20operator%20MTN,Rugby%20World%20Cup%20in%20Japan; https://www.news24.com/citypress/news/mtn-holds-on-to-springbok-sponsorship-but-not-just-because-of-the-world-cup-20191108; https://www.facebook.com/springboks/posts/be-the-bozza-with-the-mtn-and-the-boksmtn-the-official-team-sponsor-of-the-sprin/10155764656179576/; https://www.springboks.rugby/news-features/articles/2019/06/05/mtn-to-send-bok-fans-to-japan/

3 https://www.forbes.com/sites/elizabethdoerr/2018/01/28/rolex-sweeps-2018-australian-open-finals-thanks-to-roger-federer-and-caroline-wozniacki/?sh=7859200127a6; https://www.sportspromedia.com/news/rolex-renews-australian-open-partnership; https://www.watchpro.com/rolex-kicks-off-first-season-as-partner-to-all-four-grand-slams-at-australian-open/; https://www.watchpro.com/rolex-closes-grand-slam-tennis-majors-adds-us-open-deals-wimbledon-australian-open/

4 https://www.driftmasters.gp/about-us/; https://www.driftmasters.gp/2020/03/19/liqui-moly-and-dmec-announce-2020-season-partnership/; https://www.liqui-moly.com/en/company/sponsoring.html; https://www.liqui-moly.com/en/ca/company/sponsoring/motorsports/formula-1.html

5 https://www.nwslsoccer.com/news/article/nwsl-announces-2020-challenge-cup-presented-by-pg-and-secret; https://www.sportsbusinessdaily.com/Daily/Issues/2019/09/16/Marketing-and-Sponsorship/PG-NWSL.aspx; https://www.bizjournals.com/cincinnati/news/2019/09/16/p-g-buying-thousands-of-tickets-to-boost-women-s.html; https://www.bizjournals.com/cincinnati/news/2019/07/15/p-g-steps-up-advertising-game-on-equal-pay-for.html

6 https://theconversation.com/when-the-poor-sponsor-the-rich-rwanda-and-arsenal-fc-97330#:~:text=Rwanda%20keeps%20surprising.,be%20a%20committed%20Arsenal%20fan; https://www.pambazuka.org/human-security/foreign-aid-rwanda-suffering-rwandans-and-congolese; https://www.theafricareport.com/16937/rwandan-tourism-scores-big-after-arsenal-deal-despite-criticism/; https://www.sportbusiness.com/news/visit-rwanda-signs-major-psg-sponsorship-rivals-existing-arsenal-deal/; https://www.newtimes.co.rw/news/10-things-know-about-rwanda-psg-deal

7 https://crickettimes.com/2020/08/ipl-title-sponsors-and-their-year-wise-fee-from-2008-to-2020/; https://about.dream11.in/News/bcci-announces-dream11-as-official-partner-of-vivo-indian-premier-league-ipl

8 https://www.sportbusiness.com/news/unibet-takes-three-year-psg-extension-to-new-territories/?registered_metered=1; https://www.kindredgroup.com/news--insights/2020/how-frances-innovative-sponsorship-models-can-help-relieve-grass-roots-sports/; https://igamingbusiness.com/fdj-to-sponsor-100-amateur-clubs-across-france/

References

Copeland, R., Frisby, W., & McCarville, R. (1996). Understanding the sport sponsorship process from a corporate perspective. *Journal of Sport Management, 10*(1), 32–48.

Crompton, J. (2004). Conceptualization and alternate operationalizations of the measurement of sponsorship effectiveness in sport. *Leisure Studies, 23*(3), 267–281.

IEG (2018). Signs point to healthy sponsorship spending in 2018. https://www.sponsorship.com/Report/2018/01/08/Signs-Point-To-Healthy-Sponsorship-Spending-In-201.aspx

Kuzma, J.R., & Shanklin, W.L. (1994). Corporate sponsorship: An application for analysis. In Graham, P.J. (Ed.), *Sport business, operational and theoretical aspects* (pp. 82–87). Madison, WI: Brown and Benchmark.

Mullin, B.J., Hardy, S., & Sutton, W.A. (2007). *Sport marketing.* Champaign, IL: Human Kinetics.

O'Reilly, N., & Madill, J. (2009). Methods and metrics in sponsorship evaluation. *Journal of Sponsorship, 2*(3), 215–230.

Schwarz, E., & Hunter, J. (2018). *Advanced theory and practice in sport marketing.* London: Routledge.

3 Sport sponsorship activation

Activation 101

Industry-wide consensus is that sponsorship today is much more than logo placement or having an athlete use your product. Global market research firms publish studies daily that show that activation beyond the association between the sponsor and property is the key to success in sponsorship. And, as you read in Chapter 2, brands seek to achieve hundreds of different objectives through sponsorship, drawing on a variety of tactics and platforms to pursue the achievement of these objectives.

Sponsorship activation "refers to the additional investment and activity in a sponsorship beyond the rights fee spent to initially acquire a property" (O'Reilly & Lafrance-Horning, 2014, p. 425). If done well, activation is known to allow a brand to reach target markets through the cluttered promotional marketplaces of today, to aid against ambush marketing (i.e., competitors of the brand seeking to undermine their sponsorships of attractive sport properties), and to enable differentiation of the sponsor brand from it competition.

Thus, it is clear to anyone in sponsorship that to realize the full potential of any sponsorship, the sponsor and the property both need to invest in sponsorship activation. Since, as noted, sponsorship activation is the practice of investing in additional marketing efforts to enhance sponsorship effectiveness, the insight here is that brands and properties need to spend additional resources beyond the rights fee to execute different tactics, including marketing communication efforts and promotional activities. The case study below (Case study 3.1) of Toyota and the Australian Football League highlights a sponsorship partnership that includes a series of activations to maximize its effectiveness, including raffles, promotions, charitable initiatives, and specialized kits, mostly at the community level in Australia.

DOI: 10.4324/9781003154631-3

Case study 3.1 Toyota and the Australian Football League[1]

In 2019, the AFL and Toyota signed a four-year extension to their sponsorship deal, which will bring the partnership to its 20th anniversary in 2023. The deal is worth $18.5 million per year, for a total of $74 million, an upgrade over the previous $16 million per year deal. This deal is also the largest sports sponsorship deal in Australian corporate history, and makes the AFL the highest-earning sporting body from sponsorship in the country (over Tennis Australia). The deal also expands Toyota's naming rights, making Toyota a naming partner for the National Volunteer Awards, the National Inclusion Carnival, the North East Australian Football League (NEAFL), and the National Wheelchair Championships, as well as making it an official partner of the women's AFLW competition.

"Our partnership started in 2004 and over that time the contribution Toyota has made to footy, not only the AFL but at a community level, is nothing short of amazing" (Gillon McLachlan, AFL CEO). Through the Good For Footy program, Toyota has raised more than $5.7 million for grassroots football since it began in 2008, and aimed to raise $1 million in 2019 to help more than 1,000 local, grassroots AFL clubs add better facilities and equipment.

In response to the pandemic-induced pause of the AFL regular scheduling, Toyota promoted the resumption of the AFL season in June with the We Bounce Back initiative, showcasing the resilience, passion, and unity of football in Australia. Toyota also continued its Good For Footy raffle and merchandise sales, raising funds for grassroots football during the pandemic. They also sponsored apparel kits for 100 women's teams, providing apparel specifically designed for female athletes.

The activation ratio

Activation can be described as the practice of implementing different efforts, including marketing communications, hospitality, and customer experiences, in order to add value and support a sponsorship and enhance its effectiveness. To enhance a sponsorship's effectiveness, one has to spend additional resources beyond the rights fee to execute different marketing communication efforts.

You may ask, how much should be added and in what ways? The activation ratio (O'Reilly & Lafrance-Horning, 2013) is widely viewed as the way to do this. Quite simply, it refers to the incremental spend beyond the rights fee by a sponsor to give life and value to its sponsorship engagement. To illustrate, if Alibaba is paying USD$100 million to the Olympic Games as an official sponsor, the USD$100 million sponsorship fee is only to acquire the official right of association with the Games. In order to further communicate and publicize its official association with the Games, Alibaba has to make an extra investment in additional marketing and communications effort. These can include but are not limited to outdoor signage at the Games, online content around the Games, social media, digital communications, the Alibaba website, the IOC website, print, television, streaming, and radio. Further, Alibaba may create a new joint social media platform with the Games or sponsor a Olympians around the world to be able to further communicate their sponsorship via those athletes in their home countries. This mix of traditional and innovative activations allows sponsors to reach different market segments in many places. All these mediums might be implemented – for example, in the case of the Olympic sponsors such as Alibaba – in various countries around the world. They may decide to activate in more than 100 countries around the world to communicate and publicize their sponsorship of the Olympic Games. The activations they select need to be the best ways to reach, interact, engage and impact audiences of the sport property who also could be audiences of the sponsor. In the case of Alibaba and the Olympic Games, the overlap is considerable, and the importance of the activation is clear. Activation helps consumers differentiate between a sponsor and one of its competitors, assists the sponsor to break through promotional clutter, aids to effectively maximize return on investment for the sponsor, and enables meaningfully achievement of the higher stages of sponsorship objectives (see Chapter 2), including image transfer and sales.

The activation ratio is the ratio of the additional activation investment to the cost of the rights fees. In other words, it is a way to measure the extent of activation on a given sponsorship, where every dollar spent on activation increases the ratio. For major sponsors with active sponsors, the activation ratio can go as high as 7:1, even 10:1 in odd cases (O'Reilly & Lafrance-Horning, 2013). In these situations, activation costs much more than the rights fee that the sponsor paid for official association to the sport property. The recommended ratio varies across academic and industry publications, with a range of results from less than 1:1 to as high as 10:1, as noted earlier. IEG measures the activation ratio in the United States annually, with the most recent assessments at 2.1:1 (IEG, 2019) and the Canadian Sponsorship Landscape Study (2020) measured Canada at a much lower 0.58:1, or 58 cents on the dollar. These studies, however, are industry wide, and include sponsorships with very little activation, often smaller ones. In academic studies, focused on brands who are active in their marketing, these numbers are often higher. A rule of thumb we often put forward is that you should activate *at least* 1:1. Yet, clearly, there cannot be a set ratio that is common to any sponsorship; in fact, the expectation is that the activation will vary considerably from sponsorship to sponsorship. As a result, it is difficult to suggest a ratio without taking the full understanding of a sponsorship into consideration. For example, multinational companies such as Coca-Cola sponsoring an Olympic Games may spend on activation ten times the fee that they paid to acquire a sponsorship. Whereas a local coffee shop sponsoring a high school football team may spend less on activation than the amount paid for sponsorship rights fees.

The importance of activation

Regardless of the activation ratio, sponsorship without activation is a donation with no expectation for a commercial return on investment. In the case of sponsorship investment without activation, it may even end up being unproductive. Hence, effective sponsorship requires effective activation to generate a return on sponsorship investment for a brand.

AUTHORS' BLOG: ACTIVATE OR ABDICATE

If you are not going to activate your sponsorships, you might as well buy advertising. Because sponsorship without activation is pretty much like sports without fans, and during the COVID-19 pandemic, we all learned all too well what a "blah" that feeling is.

There are numerous data-validated reasons why you should activate your sponsorships, but simply put, it increases ROI. Well-activated sponsorships increase the ROI for both the brand (sponsor) and the property (sponsee). You have heard about the concept of win-win, so this seems logical so far.

But for some reason, there is a reluctance among some to activate. Perhaps, it is a lack of budget, in which case the brand should have acquired a less pricey partnership. Maybe, it is a lack of experience, in which case, the brand should hire an agency or lean on the property for support. Perhaps, it lacks conviction, in which case we would encourage any brand to read on because we will convince you why you should activate.

Let us start with fundamental reframing. Activation confuses people. They think the term applies only to the period during which the event or game is happening, when, in fact, the term activation implies that the sponsorship is active. In simple terms, that means when the games are happening.

But nothing could be farther from the truth. Your sponsorship marketing plan needs to be alive when your consumer is engaging with the sport. As you know, the consumer, or fan, is involved with their sport, team, and heroes on a 24/7 basis.

Thus, perhaps we should think of *activation as the engagement plan*. Now, the fun will start. Now, you can pretend that you are shadowing the #1 fan of your sponsorship and begin to imagine all of the opportunities, locations, and occasions to intersect with them. This approach should be straightforward because the probability is high that you are a fan as well.

The engagement plan you create is akin to a customer journey. For today's marketers, the customer journey is a de facto mandatory component of any marketing strategy. Does your event have a customer journey?

So grab a pencil and map the journey. Create five to seven phases or periods to interact. The final stage will loop back into the first phase because the customer journey is a flywheel, not a runway. Each step energizes the next, and the final stage accelerates the first phase for another cycle.

Close to the end of your journey is the event. It is usually two or three phases before the final step in each cycle. But the final step is misleading because the last becomes the first.

OK, enough of this circular argument. Let's map this out. Here is the journey.

Phase 1 – This is the need phase. At this point, the consumer has an unfulfilled need. A desire to raise money, attend a game, support their team, or participate in an event.

Phase 2 – Along comes the event or opportunity to fulfill their need. Usually, the customer becomes aware of the chance from advertising or word of mouth. If, for example, it is a sporting event, it is the first time they hear about it.

Phase 3 – This is the consideration phase. The consumer is deciding if they will buy tickets, enter the marathon, or plan the trip. They could also determine how they want to consume the event. In simple terms, will they attend it live? Watch it at a public venue, sports bar? Go to a friend's to watch? Or watch at home?

Phase 4 – Now, the customer is ready to commit. Perhaps in the consideration phase, they had various purchase options. The hard part is choosing, but now they need to choose, buy, register, and commit.

Phase 5 – This is often one of the neglected steps. Because the consumer has declared their intentions, brands can engage with them by offering programs for the running event they have signed up for, preview publications that talk about the big tournament they are going to watch, fan merchandise to flaunt on the way to the big game – you name it.

Phase 6 – Game Day. Sponsors do this every day, and they often do it quite horribly. Sorry, but it is true. But this is the opportunity to leverage the excitement of the game to market your product.

Phase 7 – The "morning after awareness" phase for engagement is the first phase you should curate postevent. How will you engage with the fans of the winning team? How will you help the first-time marathoner celebrate their accomplishment? How will you thank the volunteer who has put in so many hours? More importantly, how will you sign them up to do it all again with your event? Or your brand and your sponsorship engagement?

Reread these seven phases. Notice something? Your sponsorship programs now feel alive. No longer does it seem static, or linear, or soulless. Sponsorship activation is not a dirty word, and it is an opportunity to create magic and a chance to provide value to your customers. It is time to generate ROI.

Activation as the engagement plan

As we put in our blog and have discussed thus far in the chapter, activation is essential to any sponsorship. Without it, success is not possible, which is the key insight to take away.

In the blog, we proposed considering activation as an engagement plan. So we are taking our own advice and outlining here what that means.

First, let us start with the goals of the sponsor, the return-on-sponsorship as we have been calling it. These are really the core of determining the success of a sponsorship and if renewal will occur in the future. As you learned in the previous two chapters, sponsors have hundreds of specific objectives that they seek with sponsorship. We grouped these under four categories in Chapter 2, namely, awareness/exposure, understanding/knowledge, liking/image, and reciprocity/sales. As mentioned above, those sponsors who activate are likely to be most successful in achieving their objectives and protect against the competition and drive differentiation. During major events, it is common to observe nonsponsors (i.e., the competitors of official sponsors) using creative strategies to undermine the effectiveness in reaching its objectives of an official sponsor (their competitor). The competitors also attempt to take advantage of the attention, goodwill, and other benefits associated with a major sport property, such as the Olympic Games. In this regard, activation helps clarify any possible confusion consumers may have as to who is the official sponsor of a property.

An example of a sponsor (Burger King in the UK) using activation to engage with a specific audience (fans of the Stevenage Football Club) is outlined in Case study 3.2.

Case study 3.2 The Burger King Stevenage Challenge (2019)[2]

The Stevenage Football Club (based in the town of Stevenage, England) is not known for its on-field performance. In fact, it is one of the UK's least performing clubs. That said, it has a large online following, which is what attracted Burger King. The Stevenage Challenge consisted of a series of football challenges for fans, rewarding participants with free Burger King menu favorites, with the goal of turning Stevenage into the biggest FC in the online world. Fans complete challenges from simply scoring a goal to scoring direct from a corner. They all do these while wearing a Burger King–sponsored Stevenage FC shirt. Fans then upload and share a video of completing their challenge to claim their prize. Stevenage FC CEO, Alex Tunbridge, spoke to their partnership with Burger King as a partnership that demonstrates a property does not necessarily need to be a big football club, at all times, to think big when it comes to innovation and presence.

As a result of the sponsorship, Stevenage FC became the most used team in FIFA 20 Career Mode. Following the initial stages of the Stevenage challenge, Burger King challenged FIFA players around the world to choose Stevenage FC when playing online or in Career Mode and share video clips of their goals online to receive rewards from Burger King. This led to more than 25,000 goals shared online, and Stevenage shirts selling out for the first time in history. The initiative also received praise from a number of popular personalities on social media, including Piers Morgan, calling it "world class marketing" by putting international stars such as Messi, Ronaldo, and Neymar Jr. in Burger King Stevenage FC jerseys in FIFA 20.

It is reported that this deal was in the six-figure realm, quite small compared to the eight-figure deals that companies sign for clubs such as Real Madrid – not a small deal considering the fact that Stevenage Challenge became popular in the UK, Brazil, and the United States, and across Europe.

As with any planning process, sponsors and properties are advised to assess and identify potential activation opportunities prior to the sponsorship as part of an engagement plan approach. In today's environment, as we emerge from COVID-19, it is also advisable for sponsors to rethink current sponsorship investments, unless new, creative, and unique activations emerge. As mentioned above, properties need to have a well-articulated understanding of their own assets, which will enable them to develop, innovate, and offer activation ideas to their sponsor partners. Case study 3.3 describes a highly engaged set of activations in a particular partnership.

Case study 3.3 Nike and Chinese Tencent League of Legends Pro League[3]

In 2019, Nike signed a four-year deal with the Chinese Tencent LoL Pro League (a professional league for League of Legends in China) to provide apparel for all teams and sell merchandise. The deal made Nike to be the exclusive apparel and footwear provider for the league up to 2022. Additionally, Nike will explore new physical training programs customized for esports athletes. Bobby Jin, Co-CEO of TJ Sports – a joint venture between

Tencent and Riot Games – said in a statement, "The partnership with Nike can bring more professional and scientific services to esports athletes". The deal also made Nike the first traditional sportswear company to secure top partner designation for the TJ Sports venture. The deal is reportedly worth approximately USD$7.5 million per year. Nike reportedly beat out Adidas and the Chinese brand 361° for the partnership. Within the 2019 season alone, TJ Sports announced nine sponsorship deals in addition to Nike, including Mercedes-Benz, KFC, L'Oréal, and Alienware.

Prior to the deal, Nike had collaborated with one of the league's star players, Jian "Uzi" Zihao, as part of an advertising campaign. The mini documentary also featured NBA star LeBron James. At the time of the mini documentary, Nike's local competitor in China, Li-Ning, provided apparel for the Newbee esports team. The LoL deal with Nike may have been Nike's attempt to gain apparel exclusivity within the up-and-coming esports global phenomenon, along with the various activations implemented.

It is worth mentioning here that the third key stakeholder in sponsorship, the agency, often takes a leadership role in activation, including developing and implementing engagements. Often, for a major activation, multiple agencies are involved, including talent agencies (access to celebrity athletes, coaches, national team athletes, etc.), creative agencies (develop the digital and print content to share), sponsorship agencies (ideate and build out the activation options), and ad agencies (provide the media platforms).

Activation methods

At this point, hopefully, it is clear that activation is important and must be designed carefully. If we are at that point, the key question now moves to, "How?" and more specifically, "How do we activate?" Fortunately, a series of activation methods have been employed by sponsors, properties, and their agencies over the years, and a number of industry and academic researchers have looked closely at these activation methods. Since there are so many different activations out there, we grouped them into a series of nine categories under the two larger themes: standard and value-added activations.

It is important to recognize that no particular activation method is more effective than another across all sponsorships. Rather, in executing each of the methods, one has to make sure that any chosen activation aligns with, and allows the sponsor to achieve the objectives it has set out for the given sponsorship. Indeed, by establishing an activation program based on clearly laid-out sponsorship objectives, the ability to develop unique and creative sponsorship activation initiatives can emerge, provided that sufficient resources need to be allocated for their execution. These resources include human resources, time, and financial budget. Even if only a lower budget or resource base is possible, and if this is known upfront, the creation of activation initiatives within the allocated budget can take place. The activation ratio concept, as you may have been thinking, makes sense here as it may potentially include spending on many different activation methods chosen by the sponsor.

Figure 3.1 presents the nine different categories of activation methods, which will be described in more detail in the pages that follow.

The nine activation method categories in Figure 3.1 include five methods under the "standard" list and another four under the "value-added" category. The standard five activation methods represent those which have traditionally been part of sponsorship, and that have been predominately, but not always, exercised in the offline context. The

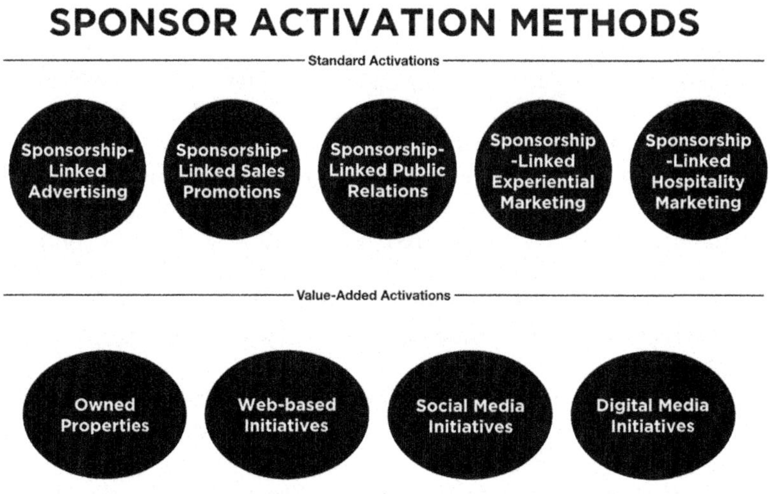

SPONSOR ACTIVATION METHODS

──────── Standard Activations ────────

- Sponsorship-Linked Advertising
- Sponsorship-Linked Sales Promotions
- Sponsorship-Linked Public Relations
- Sponsorship-Linked Experiential Marketing
- Sponsorship-Linked Hospitality Marketing

──────── Value-Added Activations ────────

- Owned Properties
- Web-based Initiatives
- Social Media Initiatives
- Digital Media Initiatives

Figure 3.1 Activation Methods.

value-added methods include those that are more recent in their construction, often with digital components, and that are innovative in their ability to support the achievement of sponsor objectives. Notably, as time goes by, all of these methods are becoming increasingly digital in nature.

All five of the standard methods and the four value-added methods can be executed offline and online. For example, a sponsorship-linked advertising activation can be conducted on social media platforms through postings where a discounted ticket to a sport event is offered only to those who purchase the products/services of the sponsor online. Similarly, a sponsor could bring a popular player to a school in a low-income neighborhood for a live coaching session shared on YouTube.

Standard activations

Standard activation practices refer to those traditional activation initiatives that have been part of sponsorship for many years and that are typically conducted offline, although as time goes on, they include increasingly digital components. The most important insight for you to take away from this set of activation methods is that these are the methods that are expected by a sponsor and thus should be included. For a property offering activation opportunities, these standard activations should not be viewed as innovative or creative or as "special" in terms of how they will be perceived by the sponsor. Each of these methods, along with corresponding examples, is discussed in the following sections.

Sponsorship-linked advertising. The utilization of an advertising campaign that thematically includes the imagery of a sport property by the sponsor is what this activation method involves. Simply defined, advertising is a form of one-way mass communication about a product/service. It is normally a noninteractive and nonpersonal communication that is not tailored to individuals. Sponsorship-linked advertising enhances awareness of a sponsor's association by highlighting the property-brand partnership. The advertisement can be communicated in association with the property's name, logo, font type, symbols, color, and shape. The use of athletes (participating in a sport property), in particular in sponsorship-linked advertisements, is an effective approach. Sometimes, coaches, diehard fans, or other stakeholders are used.

Sponsorship-linked advertisements can be carried through different outlets such as outdoor (billboard, poster, fliers), print (newspaper and magazine coverages and ads), radio, television (coverage and commercials), property-themed giveaways (e.g., pins, pens, keyholders), property-branded products (e.g., branded uniforms, cars, office supplies), and property-related marketing themes (e.g., Emirates Airlines relating its "Fly Better" marketing campaign to a sponsored property). Placing newspaper advertisements or newspaper inserts featuring participating athletes around the time of the sponsorship is one example of this method. Other approaches such as sponsorship-linked roadshows (i.e., a series of events [often a day or less in length] that are held in different locations [typically cities] over a period of time, such as the summer months) can also be considered as activation through traditional advertising.

The case study below outlines some challenges due to a poor launch of the new sponsorship. It is about a sponsorship based largely on sponsorship-linked activations, in the form of a logo on the jerseys of a football club.

Case study 3.4 South African Football Association, shifting from Nike to Le Coq Sportif[4]

Following the conclusion of a five-year deal with Nike ending with concluded following the 2019 Africa Cup of Nations, the South African Football Association (SAFA) was in need of an apparel sponsor. With four potential sponsors on the table, including Nike, SAFA was looking to address concerns with their Bafana (the national soccer team) shirt. In December 2019, SAFA's acting CEO admitted that the Bafana jersey was not one of the most popular national team jerseys available, and that the organization would look to improve on this with new sponsors. Additionally, price and accessibility were cited as issues with the shirt, which had led to reduced sales during the deal with Nike. "In an ideal world we'll have a sponsor that will have a footprint throughout the country. It should be possible for anyone anywhere to have the shirt" (in the words of Gay Mokoena, SAFA former acting CEO).

In October 2020, SAFA signed a new five-year deal with the French apparel company, Le Coq Sportif. However, this activation was anything but smooth. Without prior communication to stakeholders, SAFA announced over Twitter their deal with the apparel company in a "clumsy video." The national team wore the jerseys for the first time with mixed reactions from the players, with one stating that they did not even know there was a new kit sponsor until the week after the deal was signed. Danny Jordann, SAFA president, defended the decision. Le Coq agreed to put the star (AFCON 1996 triumph) on the jersey, a nod to past successes of the team and an inspiration to the future. Also, with production of the kit taking place in South Africa, Jordann believed the partnership would bring jobs to South Africans over the course of the deal.

Sponsorship-linked public relations. The activations are conducted for the good of the general public and covered by the media as a third-party endorsement of the good deed with the objective of being noticed by those interested in the sponsored sport property. Simply defined, public relations refer to a company's intentionally scheduled public events aimed to show community support in a way that it attracts media coverage, where the coverage is presented (and is perceived) as news and not an advertisement by the public. For example, in a case of cause-related tie-in, a sponsor may set up donation boxes at different corners of the property's venue, and encourage people to donate sport gear for children in Africa with a chance to be entered into a prize draw for a VIP experience. Another example is when a sponsor simultaneously sponsors another property in a different area such as arts, science, culture, or education, then timing the promotions of both sponsorships to be at the same time and with related messaging, thus presenting the cause-related initiatives as an extension of the sport sponsorship. Comparably, a sponsor may decide to build basketball courts or hockey rinks, upgrade a city park, and inaugurate them coinciding with the launch of a sport sponsorship in the same market. The sponsor offering their employees the opportunity to volunteer for the sport property and providing them a branded T-shirt to wear can also be considered as a sponsorship-linked public relations activation.

Sponsorship-linked sales promotions. The activations are different short-term incentives that are often used by a sponsor to stimulate immediate demand for a product or service. A sponsorship-linked sales promotion seeks to entice audiences to action, such as promised offers and incentives that help drive short-term sales. For instance, sponsors can set up *shops at venues, execute in-venue promotions, and undertake in-store promotions*. While setting up kiosks at a venue is the most commonly used sponsorship-linked sales promotion activation, some typical examples of in-venue promotions include giving away property-themed products of a sponsor to attendees, including bobbleheads, bags, T-shirts, hats, autographs, retail coupons, and towels. Sponsors may also sponsor mini events within the larger sport property, such as kids' night, family day, or half-time of a college game.

In-store sales promotions can help a sponsor drive potential consumers to a sponsor's retail or online stores. In-store promotional tactics associated with a sponsorship can include discounts, coupons, sweepstakes, prizes, and discounts. Example include (i) being entered into a lottery draw when a customer buys a ticket to a sport property (e.g., win an air ticket from an airline sponsor), (ii) offering free product for buyers who enter in and win a property-themed contest (e.g., the first three months' free talk time from a telecom company), (iii) extending lower interest rates for those buying tickets (e.g., new credit card customers from a bank sponsor), (iv) offering bonuses (e.g., collecting points if a customer uses a sponsor's products and/or services), (v) providing a free host city tour coupon for those ordering a product, and (vi) providing a chance to win a VIP experience for those who buy a sponsor's product and/or service. Another example is developing and selling event-themed products/services around the time of the sponsored property (e.g., event-themed credit card).

Sponsorship-linked experiential marketing. The activations are on-site special activities or "on-the-ground" marketing activities. Sponsorship-linked experiential marketing is about creating a face-to-face or a real-life memorable experience for customers of a sport property. The on-the-ground experience engages event attendees to experience the sponsor's offerings, which, by extension, allows these spectators, participants, or supporters to have a firsthand interaction with the product and/or service. For example, Samsung sets up booths at the Olympic Games' venues and athletes' villages to allow athletes, coaches, spectators, and other visitors to interact with and experience its products, such as virtual reality technology. Sponsorship-linked experiential marketing can also provide attendees an opportunity to interact with the sponsor's brand representatives, which allows attendees to ask questions and learn about a product through a one-on-one dialogue. This kind of interaction can be very effective as it allows the brand representative to explain every dimension of a sponsor's product and answer all of the potential customer's questions through focused and concentrated attention. These interactions can set the stage to establish a long-term relationship.

Activations based on sponsorship-linked experiential marketing can be powerful ways to generate meaningful connections between a sponsor and followers of the sport property. These experiential activities have the potential to generate consumer ties to a sponsor and have the potential to impact consumer behavior in a meaningful way. Hence, it is essential that the experience (that is part of the activation) is relevant, entertaining, subtly educational, and engaging. While this activation method most effectively facilitates the accomplishment of the last two stages of sponsorship objectives (namely image/liking and reciprocity/sales), it can also be an ideal approach to introduce new products or services.

Sponsorship-linked hospitality marketing. These activations are about providing entertainment opportunities through the sport property to the sponsor's employees, partners, suppliers, investors board members, shareholders, brokers, distributors, retailers, customers, and potential customers via the assets provided in the sponsorship package. Both business-to-business (B2B) and business-to-consumer (B2C) marketing efforts can include these activations. For example, providing a VIP experience to key business partners is B2B, while one for high value potential customers is B2C.

Sponsorship-linked hospitality marketing activations may also include activities such as meeting players, offering accreditation to an event, or providing access to a VIP-only area, to further heighten the hospitality experience. An example is when a sponsor provides free parking to all attendees, and communicates the offer in a number of different ways, such as distributing a parking ticket with the printed message, "XYZ welcomes you to the event and we cover your parking. Enjoy the event and check out our website ...". Another example would be if a sponsor of a marathon were to offer a four-weekend training program led by an Olympian.

Value-added activations

As described above, the five categories of standard activation practices are those that are "common practice" in sponsorship and have been for a while. The next set, value-added activations, are those activations that are innovative, modern, often digital and that provide a sponsor with the ability to achieve their objectives. These activations are often developed by agencies on behalf of their sponsor and/or property client. We present these as a separate set of activations to encourage practitioners to put time and energy toward developing advanced initiatives outside of the standard activations. There are four categories of value-added activations discussed below. The first is the "owned property", sometimes called "branded content", which is a specific activation outside of the core sport property. The other three are based on the online platform. The online activations often involve a sponsor's effort that can be best facilitated by the online medium. These can be seen across three different domains, namely, digital media-based initiatives, web-based initiatives, and social media-based initiatives. Each of these methods, along with corresponding examples, is discussed in the following sections. Case study 3.5 discusses the global sponsor of the International Olympic Committee and the Olympic Games, Omega, and its activations around the Games.

Case study 3.5 Omega House[5]

The Olympic Games is about more than a competition. It is a megaevent and a pinnacle of global festival. OMEGA has been the official timekeeper of more than 25 Olympic Games, but also recognized as the "unofficial party champion" of the 2012 London Games with its OMEGA House activation, which was well received. This exclusive members-only club "gather[s] all the spirit and milestones of the famous Swiss brand together in one beautifully designed [...] home" (https://www.omegawatches. com/en-us/stories/omega-house-in-rio). OMEGA House happened around the 2016 Rio Games as well.

The house is temporary location on the ground at a Games. The interior design of the 2012 version reflects and is inspired by OMEGA's brand and product history. For example, a kinetic diver installation in the main lobby paid homage to the brand's diving heritage, and the Speedmaster Room was inspired by OMEGA's creation of the first NASA-approved watch to be worn to the moon, featuring a visit from famous astronaut Buzz Aldrin. The opening of OMEGA House in London, and throughout the duration of the 2012 Games, featured the attendance of many athletes, coaches, and celebrities. For instance, Hollywood stars Eddie Redmayne and Nicole Kidman were the first two to sign OMEGA's Wall of Fame at the 2012 Games. Following the conclusion of the 2012 Games, the location was converted into a permanent OMEGA boutique, the largest in Europe.

Owned Properties. Also known as "branded content", these activations are known to be exceptionally effective if done correctly. They can be digital and in-person in nature, with their key defining characteristics being (i) that they are jointly created by the brand and the property outside of the core sport property to enhance its effectiveness and (ii) that they allow the sponsor to activate without many of the restrictions faced in a direct sponsorship of a sport property (access to athletes, clean venue limited signage, etc.). An illustrative example is one that has been launched by Fortune 500 food manufacturer Kraft in both Canada and the United States as part of its sponsorships with the NHL. The activations are called "Kraft Hockeyville", where communities – in each of Canada and the United States – compete for the title of Kraft Hockeyville, where the winner (via fan voting) received an investment ($250,000 in 2019) to upgrade their local arena and coverage on a network telecast of an NHL game on NBC in the United States and the Sportsnet network in Canada. During that telecast, the crews and personalities of the networks are in the winning town and broadcast from that location around a day of festivities. Kraft benefits as millions of people vote, thousands of people join committees to try to win for their local town, and hundreds of municipalities take part. Case study 3.6 discusses product alignment in sponsorship activation: Fiat versus the Brazilian Football Confederation.

Case study 3.6 Fiat and the Brazilian Football Confederation (CBF)[6]

The CBF and Fiat signed a four-year deal in 2019 which will see Fiat sponsor the men's, women's, and youth level soccer programs of the CBF until the end of the Qatar World Cup in 2022. "The bond with Fiat is highly strategic and comes at an important moment for Brazil's national teams", said Rogério Caboclo, CBF president. The deal covered many important competitions in the international football schedule: Women's World Cup (France), Copa América Brasil 2019, Copa America 2020, Tokyo Olympics (Japan), and the 2022 World Cup in Qatar. At the time the deal was signed, the financial terms were not announced.

"The shirt of the Brazilian national team is known all over the world, as well as the Fiat logo and products. Both seek talent and are two brands that combine tradition and innovation", said Rogério Caboclo, CBF president. Fiat's Latin America president, Antonio Filosa said the sponsorship joins "two great passions of our country, football and cars." In addition to the deal with the CBF, Fiat also has shirt sponsorships with two Brazilian clubs, Atlético Mineiro and Cruzeiro. A large component of the deal's activation included the release of a limited Fiat Argo series. Limited to 1,500 units, the car is a tribute from Fiat to the partnership with CBF. The cars are available in yellow or blue (like the teams jerseys) and can come with exclusive stickers to represent the Brazilian teams. Fiat executives spoke to the qualities of the car in a similar fashion as one would an elite athlete. The Fiat team also put the product together in a short two-month time frame once the sponsorship deal had been announced.

Digital media activation initiatives. These are activations that are focused on the modern and ever shifting use technology in sponsorship. Here, we define digital media as any form of media that uses electronic devices for distribution. The commonly used elements of digital media for sponsorship activation include apps, augmented reality (AR), virtual reality (VR), podcasts, audiobooks, video games, DVD, and CD-ROM. Digital media devices are usually engaging and easy to use; thus, the use of digital devices for sponsorship activation requires creative approaches and consideration of the fast-changing landscape of available and emerging digital devices.

Importantly, in designing digital media activation initiatives, a sponsor can be limited only by one's creativity and imagination. To provide some insights, examples of sponsorship activation using augmented reality (AR), virtual reality (VR), and apps are provided here. In terms of using AR for sponsorship activation, the AT&T and Dallas Cowboys initiative is an illustrative example. AT&T (the Cowboys' stadium naming rights sponsor), in partnership with Dallas Cowboys, enhances the fan experience in the stadium using an augmented reality (AR) photo opportunity entitled "Pose with the Pros". It is the first ever in-stadium photo booth opportunity that allows fans to select and take selfies with their favorite home players and have it sent to their smartphone immediately. This activation allowed AT&T to appeal to Cowboys' fans and help establish positive emotional connections between AT&T and potential consumers. Similarly, VR can be used to activate sponsorship, where, for example, a sponsor can provide fans with a VR opportunity to purchase tickets. In this example, fans who cannot go and check seats at a sporting venue can pick their premium seats using a 3D seating app of a stadium provided by a sponsor, where the app provides the consumer a vantage point to see the stadium from their potential seat. Another example is sport apparel manufacturer, Nike, whose digital media activations, including its Training Club App, and a running app that provides self-guided runs, allow Nike to communicate its e-commerce offerings via these digital activations. Digital activation offers a unique pathway for reaching a specific type of sponsors' target markets.

Web-based activation initiatives. These activations seek to elevate the connection between brand and sport property in an entertaining and engaging way. Often, they are creative, innovative and include (i) linking a sponsor's website to that of the sponsored property, (ii) developing a property-themed mini website, and (iii) designing sponsorship-linked web-based activities.

The first, linking a sponsor-property holder website, is a common element in most sponsorship packages, where the visitor to the sport property website is provided with the option to click on a hyperlinked logo and visit the sponsor's page that is linked. The same ideally happens on the sponsor's web, with a link to the sport property's website. Although relatively straightforward in nature, this does not always happen (permissions, effort, etc.) as often as one might think (just check out a few sponsors and property websites); but when it does, it can generate online traffic, particularly when the sport property (e.g., Manchester United) or the sponsor (e.g., Nike) has significant website activity. Notably, these links can also be done in creative ways in terms of integration and profile on the websites.

Second, mini website activations with a sport property theme can support the engagement of property-interested consumers. These can be stand-alone website (e.g., Alibaba and the IOC – https://olympics.alibabacloud.com/) or are sections of a website (e.g., Esso and Hockey Canada – https://www.essomedals.com/) that are developed in relation to a sponsored property. These are more common in properties that happen annually, like the Boston Marathon, or at regular intervals like the World Cup or the Olympic Games. These types of activations are rare but, when done effectively, can communicate impactful messages that benefit both sponsor and sport property.

Third, sponsorship-linked web-based activities are the most integrated and extensive of this set of activations, where the sponsor website and the sport property's website are linked at multiple levels. Panasonic's fita project is an illustrative example of a web-based activation used during the 2016 Rio Olympic Games. A "fita" is a kind of ribbon worn around the wrist. For the 2016 Games, Panasonic developed a special website entitled "DREAM 'FITA' PROJECT", which allowed fans to create a virtual fita online on the special website. And if an individual shared their fita on social media, they received a personalized message of support from superstar Brazilian footballer Neymar Jr. A second example is the 2008 Lenovo notebook philanthropy auction, when Lenovo, who had become a global sponsor of the Olympic Games that year, offered a series of "Cloud of Promise"-themed notebook PCs available for bidding at a website developed specifically for the auction. The limited-edition notebook PCs were autographed by Lenovo Champions – well known Olympic athletes who acted as athlete ambassadors – offering fans the opportunity to bid and own a part of Olympic history. Proceeds from the auction were donated to support organizations that support youth development in underprivileged areas of the world.

Social media activation initiatives. The unique features of social media make it a conducive medium for sponsors to communicate with consumers. These unique features are effective for sponsorship activation and include speed, easy access, real-time functioning, connectivity, and public forum. Along with these features, social media has an inherent feature of serving as a hub for users with common needs, shared passions, and mutual interest in a sport property. Social media further has the power of drawing high numbers of followers with similar interests to the platforms (e.g., Facebook, Twitter, Instagram) and, by extension, aggregating reachable target audiences of a specific sport. Activating a sponsorship on a property's social media platforms therefore allows a sponsor to access those who are responsive to marketing communication efforts around the property. In addition to the opportunity to reach target audiences who are following the property's social media platforms, a social media post can also be boosted (via paid communication) to reach new audiences on the platform, beyond those who follow the sport property. Hence, the property can use its social media platforms to help a sponsor achieve its objectives.

An early but extensive study (Abeza et al., 2014) found that Olympic sponsors use social media to achieve and activate three sponsorship objectives: (i) customer appreciation, (ii) athlete encouragement, and (ii) the promotion of products, services, and corporate image. These sponsors were also found to be using social media to celebrate victories by cheering and congratulating athletes, to create an emotional connection between the sponsor and audience. Social media was also used by these sponsors for purposes of creating awareness, informing consumers, facilitating consumer appreciation of a company's products and services, and generating sales and actual sales.

Since social media is a participatory and collaborative medium, sponsors are able to communicate directly with followers (of the sport property) by linking their brand to the property and, potentially, engaging followers. One approach for sponsors in this regard is to humanize their brand by engaging in dialogue that has a friendly tone, involves humor, and that links to the sport property's personality. The opportunity to directly communicate with consumers can also create an opportunity to build and maintain a relationship with the sport property's audiences.

As part of these activations, creative social media content can be developed to promote a sponsor, such as well-thought-out graphic design and embedded video clips. While this content can organically connect with followers, it can also be boosted with different calls-to-action, such as "like us", "follow us", "comment now", "learn more", and "share now", with the goal of creating awareness that results in impressions, shares, and likes. In order to increase likes and shares, content can be attached to these calls-to-action, such as testimonials, visit-website links, chat-now offers, and contact-us information. Similarly, to encourage purchase, content can be attached (with links) to calls-to-action such as add to cart, add to wish list, download coupon, and see related products. Further, social media tactics that can enhance the effectiveness of the activation include developing hashtags and promotional campaign messages, and communicating and reaching out to the event followers. Engagement opportunities such as a 30-second testimonial video from selected attendees about a sponsor or arranging a photo contest among attendees about their best experience with a sponsor's product or service are also recommended approaches.

Sponsor activations – insights

The above discussed nine categories of activation methods offer brands a variety of options to maximize the effectiveness of their sponsorship. In sum, we highly recommend that brands (and their agencies) use a combination of each of the activation approaches in order to realize the full potential of a sponsorship investment. Doing so will allow a sponsor to accomplish varied objectives and reach their sought target markets, which differ by sponsorship.

In addition to using an effective mix of activation methods and tactics, the parties involved in any sponsorship deal, including sport property, agencies, and sponsor, are advised to stay in regular contact after signing a contract and agreeing to a sponsorship package. This should involve discussing the design, execution, and monitoring of different activation initiatives. In doing so, the parties involved will build trust among themselves and increase the chance of a successful sponsorship (i.e., achievement of objectives) and potentially lead to renewal.

Property activation

In closing this chapter, we want to provide an insight based on the recent development in sport sponsorship, which is properties getting increasingly involved in putting resources toward activation and collaborating with a sponsor and agencies in developing specific activation tactics and approaches

By investing and participating in the sponsorship activation, a property can help a sponsor better realize the outcome of its investment, toward the achievement of its objectives. In turn, this can improve the chance of sponsorship renewal. As noted, there are many more sport properties seeking sponsors than the number of available and interested sponsors. Thus, in many cases, sport properties are in need of sponsors. In the case of small-scale sport properties who are signing or renewing sponsorship agreements each year, the investment in and collaboration with sponsors on activation is highly recommended, specifically around allocating sufficient budget for activation.

In this regard, the Canadian Sponsorship Landscape Study (2020) reported that, in the last five years, properties have started reinvesting about 10% of the rights fees (back into activation) even though their agreement might not have required them to do so. Typically, an activation fee is made by a sponsor (discussed at the begging of the chapter) as an additional investment beyond the rights fee spent to initially acquire a property. Hence, the trend in Canada implies that properties are seeking to serve as an extension to a sponsor's marketing department, and amplify their efforts and engage as a partner in activation. This is noted as a key element of many of the value-added activation methods discussed.

Furthermore, as noted above, the power of property-initiated activation with social media (e.g., Facebook, Twitter, and YouTube) may be the most efficient way to do this since social media serves as a hub to its consumers, and, by nature, gathers users with similar interest who are reachable target audiences of a specific sport. As a result, a property holder can use its social media platforms to activate a sponsor's association to its audiences.

82 *Sport sponsorship activation*

Notes

1 https://www.toyota.com.au/news/toyota-australia-and-afl-ink-new-four-year-sponsorship-deal#:~:text=Toyota%20Australia%20has%20extended%20its,partnership%20deals%20to%20%2020%20years; https://www.adnews.com.au/news/afl-inks-record-74-million-sponsorship-deal-with-toyota; https://www.theguardian.com/sport/2019/mar/15/afl-in-185m-a-year-sponsorship-deal-with-toyota-reportedly-largest-ever-in-australia; https://www.toyota.com.au/partnerships/afl-aflw; https://www.afl.com.au/news/130470/afl-and-toyota-agree-to-long-term-record-breaking-deal
2 https://www.stevenagefc.com/news/2019/october/stevenage-challenge-burger-king-sky-bet-league-two-efl-thursday-17th-october-2019/; https://www.joe.co.uk/sport/burger-king-stevenage-challenge-250365; https://inews.co.uk/sport/football/burger-king-stevenage-challenge-fifa-lionel-messi-ad-campaign-786023
3 https://www.campaignasia.com/article/esports-influencers-battle-in-their-own-asian-arena/456166; https://www.reuters.com/article/us-nike-tencent-holdings-videogames-idUSKCN1QH2IW; https://www.sportspromedia.com/news/nikes-league-of-legends-pro-league-deal; https://gambliance.com/sources-teams-in-dispute-with-tencent-over-nike-sponsorship-deal-for-lpl/
4 https://www.timeslive.co.za/sport/soccer/2019-12-07-safa-to-announce-new-technical-sponsor-after-nike-contract-ends/; https://www.news24.com/sport/soccer/bafanabafana/safa-boss-on-new-kit-sponsor-our-partnership-will-create-jobs-for-south-africans-20201009
5 https://www.omegawatches.com/en-us/stories/omega-house-in-rio; https://www.businessinsider.com/inside-the-super-exclusive-private-members-club-at-the-rio-olympics-2016-8; https://www.wallpaper.com/fashion/omega-house-opens-its-doors-during-the-london-2012-olympic-games; https://www.horbiter.com/en/omega-house-rio-2016-event-olympics/
6 https://www.sportspromedia.com/news/brazils-national-soccer-team-fiat; https://www.fcagroup.com/stories/latam/en-us/Pages/patrocinio-fiat.aspx#; https://www.insidesport.co/fiat-to-drive-brazil-football-team/; https://www.sportswallah.com/football/sports-bizz/fiat-becomes-part-of-brazil-national-team-signs-deal-to-become-official-sponsor/

References

Abeza, G., Pegoraro, A., Naraine, M.L., Séguin, B., & O'Reilly, N. (2014). Activating a global sport sponsorship with social media: An analysis of TOP sponsors, Twitter, and the 2014 Olympic Games. *International Journal of Sport Management and Marketing, 15*(3–4), 184–213.
Canadian Sponsorship Landscape Study (2020). https://www.sponsorshiplandscape.com/csls/
IEG Sponsorship Report (2019) https://www.sponsorship.com/Report.aspx
O'Reilly, N., & Lafrance-Horning, D. (2013). Leveraging sponsorship: The activation ratio. *Sport Management Review, 16*(4), 424–437.

4 Sport sponsorship servicing

Servicing: the essential tactical element of sponsorship

Following activation (Chapter 3), servicing is the second key tactical element of sponsorship. The third is sponsorship evaluation (Chapter 5). Sponsorship servicing is the practice of ensuring that each and every expectation that was agreed upon in a sponsorship contract is met. In other words, it is the fulfillment of what was promised in the sponsorship contract.

In the services marketing world, which studies the services that marketers provide to any and all industries, much thought and research goes into the servicing of clients before, during, and after a sale is made of any product and/or service. These efforts are often called, or are considered as a core component of, fulfillment or account management, where what is promised to a client is sought to be delivered. Although sometimes not the case for sponsorship, many sales-based organizations have a customer service department, a unit who takes on responsibility for servicing a client following the sale. Ranging from providing customer service over the phone to serving a dinner at a restaurant, servicing is a key component of marketing and an essential element in satisfying the intangible needs of customers. The same is true in sponsorship, where what is often described in practice as sponsorship delivery, fulfillment, or servicing involves the property (and, if relevant, their agencies) carrying out and then reporting on the requirements of the contract to their sponsor. This requires four main considerations (summarized in Figure 4.1), each of which is summarized here but built out in more detail later in the chapter.

First, in terms of the sponsorship contract, the property (or its agency representative) must ensure that each and every expectation is met (signage, access to athletes, activation platforms, logo placements, invitations to key events, hospitality, tickets, etc.) as stipulated.

DOI: 10.4324/9781003154631-4

Second, it requires the allocation by the property of the financial resources necessary to deliver on those commitments (i.e., a proportion of rights fee received from the sponsorship allocated to servicing). For example, if a sponsorship summit (e.g., a meeting of all the sponsors of the given property) is offered and included in the contract, then a budget to put on that event needs to be allocated from the sponsorship revenues earned from those sponsors.

Third, the human resources necessary must be allocated to service. This is often an area of deficiency in sponsorship servicing (O'Reilly & Huybers, 2015), where commitments go undelivered due a lack of directly responsible personnel, such as a staff, an intern, an agency, or a consultant. For example, if branded giveaways were agreed to be distributed at a sponsored property's pre-event press conference, there has to be a person responsible to make sure that the giveaways are shipped, delivered on time, brought to the press conference venue, and distributed to the attendees. This is a very basic but illustrative example showing the importance of assigning responsible personnel.

The fourth, and final, consideration is an extension beyond the expected level of servicing of the sponsorship, where the property goes above and beyond what is expected by the sponsor (extra communications, additional promotional opportunities, cocreation of value with a cosponsor, inclusions in digital platforms, etc.) to enhance sponsor satisfaction, increase the likelihood of renewal, and potentially lead to increased rights fees and/or activation spend. It is important to realize that each sponsorship package (and contract) will differ and may include many different elements, some of which may be unique and innovative. From the sport property perspective, it is important to only include elements that you can delivery on. Delivering on your promise is essential if you are hoping to have the sponsorship agreement renewed in the future and, ideally, renewed at a higher rights fee level. Therefore, it is advisable for sport properties to not overvalue their assets during negotiation, but rather to underpromise and overdeliver.

Figure 4.1 captures the essentials of sponsorship servicing.

In general, published work and industry guidance on sponsorship servicing are lacking. As an insight book, we provide in this chapter practical case and examples to illustrate this important element of sponsorship.

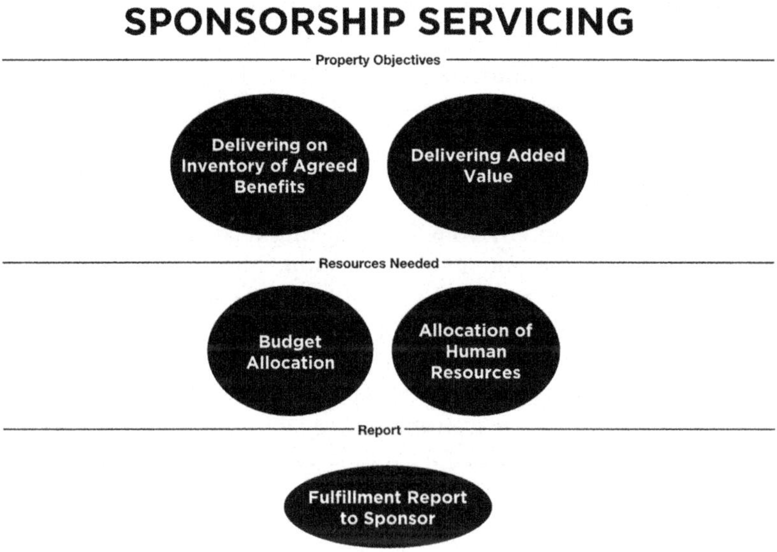

SPONSORSHIP SERVICING
Property Objectives

Delivering on Inventory of Agreed Benefits

Delivering Added Value

Resources Needed

Budget Allocation

Allocation of Human Resources

Report

Fulfillment Report to Sponsor

Figure 4.1 Sponsorship Servicing.

AUTHORS' BLOG: HELP ME HELP YOU

One of the most overlooked aspects of sponsorship servicing is a fully-fledged articulation of its role.

In fact, we would suggest that the word servicing is such a low bar that we should eradicate it from our vocabulary and suggest a better term. The job of every person in the sponsorship ecosystem is not to service it, but to enable it. Our job is to help one another to succeed. We should cocreate and innovate together. Never is this truer than from the standpoint of the property or agency in working with brand partners. In short, any property or agency should be asking how they are helping their client do their job better.

The first thing to understand is that your sponsor, we mean the person, not the company, is on your side whether you are a property or an agency. The rationale for this alliance is straightforward. Your sponsor shares a mutual desire for success with you. The more successful your property is, the more valuable their brand's relationship with your event will be. The more impactful your event is in the community, the more likely they will receive praise from their boss for being partnered with you. The more participants you have in your race, the more impact their activation will generate.

Your sponsor needs your help starting from your very first meeting about the potential partnership. At that meeting, the sponsor automatically thinks about how they will sell this concept to their company. If you approach this meeting believing your job is to sell, you are wrong. It would be best if you sold their boss on a partnership. If you are successful in securing a partnership, you should reframe your enabling (servicing) mindset. You are not just enabling your client; you are helping their entire organization.

Let us explain further and provide some insights from our experiences.

The sponsor is buying you, not your property or pitch. That first meeting is a referendum on you. Are you trustworthy? Will you be a great partner? Can I put you in front of my boss, or my board? A well-respected person can sell a defective product much more quickly than a questionable character selling bitcoin or gold or a pandemic cure, also known as a great product!

Put your Internet where your mouth is before that first meeting! We are always amazed at how many people pitch us on something – whether it be their property or themselves – and a quick scan of the Internet does not reflect their spiel. When was the last time you audited yourself and your organization's online presence? We have seen properties with three-year-old press releases on their home page, job applicants with LinkedIn profiles that do not match their resume, and their own company's website with dated case studies. Remember, the minute your sponsor prospect arranges to meet you, they are checking out your organization.

Pro tip? Lead with a great referral from a client!

You always need one more deck than planned. This piece of advice made a lot more sense 25 years ago when we went to meetings with these artifacts called briefcases, filled with these fossil-like documents called presentation decks. Back then, we loved nothing better than to whip out a new set of ideas when the meeting's original direction had hit a standstill. While it is more effortless than ever to mirror that action with digital presentations, we are not sure it is as dramatic. The real lesson here is not the format; it is the intent. If you are attending a meeting with your sponsor to discuss signage at your event, will you be prepared if they ask you for alternative ideas? You need to be. For example, what if the brand wanted to do more social media or have one of their influencers participate in the event as a guest performer, or what if they desired to integrate their CSR platform into your event. These are all realistic pivots that could happen mid-meeting, of any meeting. You, if you are as prepared as we expect you will be, want to be in a position to demonstrate that any of these activation ideas could work – with no notice. That is the idea of having an extra deck. The document could be entitled Extras, Pivots, Added Value, or Additional Options. That is servicing (enabling!) your client. The concept of thinking ahead and past the stated intention of a meeting and flexing is tremendous. You cannot go into action expecting it to follow the script. Like a great quarterback, be ready to call an audible!

From the beginning, the sponsor imagines how they will sell your opportunity to their leadership team. If your client is keen on your proposal, start the process of helping them early on. It is an old-school sales approach to ask whom they need to get approval from internally. It is a new-school sales approach to ask if you can help them prepare an internal recommendation to pitch the property. Keep that mentality throughout the relationship. Your status reports and research should provide the ammunition and tools needed to wow their internal peers about your partnership.

An inquiry from someone else has prompted every question your sponsor asks. How many times did one of your parents ask the other, or one of your siblings, to tell you something? Guess what? That does not just happen in families. It happens in business. So the next time you receive an email or text or Slack or Discord message asking for some data from your sponsor, ask who asked them (in a polite way) and, more importantly, how they like to receive information. Some parents like their breakfast in bed, and others want to eat on the deck.

Bad news becomes terrible news the longer you wait to share it. This idea could be the essential rule of sponsorship servicing/enablement. It is mandatory for you to let everyone involved know about issues the minute they happen. Mark shares that he has had doses of everything at his events over the years: three deaths, two near deaths, several scary car accidents, injuries from flying tents, no show performers, hailstorms, fights, temperamental performers, angry sponsors, poor staff, theft, missing bike racks, sleepy volunteers, low turnout, you name it. Whether it be a life-or-death emergency or a slow, painful realization that a plan will not be successful, you must communicate the issues. Early. Often. Honestly. That approach, coupled with a clear recovery plan, will save you in the long run: short-term pain, long-term gain.

Let us finish with an important story from Mark.

"My favourite job in university was bartending. Bartenders make tips at nearly every sale, well we did in that era because most people paid cash. But the difference between some loose change or a deliberate gratuity and a weekend-making monster tip was quite simple. When my service was good, I received great tips. When I enabled people to have the best night ever, my gratuities were the best. I have always said that if my business ever collapses, I will go back to bartending and earn enough money to get it back into the sponsorship game. Both jobs have the same nature as each demand and thrive on exceptional service!"

The importance of sponsorship servicing

In Chapter 3, we established the importance of activation to sponsorship effectiveness. In turn, the significance of servicing is quite clear, both in terms of its role in overall fulfillment (i.e., delivery of what was promised in the sponsorship contract) as well as its interrelated role with both activation and evaluation. A well-serviced contract by the property is vital to effectively support achieving a sponsor's pre-established objective(s). Indeed, the purpose of sponsorship servicing is to enable the sponsor's fulfillment of their objectives, whether it be sales-related (e.g., total sales, volume of sales, market share), brand-related (e.g., visibility, image transfer, brand equity, image enhancement), or hospitality-based (entertaining suppliers, distributors, retailers, etc.).

For the sport property itself, a well-serviced sponsorship can provide a number of benefits, including:

• Delivering against sponsorship objectives
• Delivering what the property promised to the brand

- Demonstrating what the property can deliver to other potential sponsors
- Validating the true promotional potential of the property
- Justifying a sponsor's investment in the property
- Providing evidence to renegotiate a sponsorship fee
- Informing discussions on the topic of renewing the sponsorship deal
- Addressing internal accountability requirements of the sponsor

Elements of sponsorship servicing

In servicing any sponsorship, there are roles that each stakeholder (brand, property, and agency) typically take on to ensure that the contractual demands of the sponsor are met. While the degree of their responsibility varies in servicing a sponsorship, each stakeholder has an important role to play in the effective delivery of a sponsorship, including the elements noted in Figure 4.1. Of note, the resource-based elements in Figure 4.1 – budget and human resources - are essential for the meaningful servicing of a sponsorship by a sport property. The allocation of these resources will vary depending on how important the sponsorship is to the property and how well the property prepares presponsorship to undertake the servicing element. In the case of a prepared property who has prioritized servicing, a focus on the three remaining elements of sponsorship servicing is advised, namely, the fulfillment of the contractual commitments, the delivery of added value beyond the committed deliverables, and the providing of a fulfillment report.

Fulfillment of the contractual commitments

Servicing sponsorship starts with the fulfillment of contractual obligations or ensuring that each and every element is met. This aspect is core to servicing in sponsorship. For this to occur, a property has to follow three sequential steps:

i   Review the sponsorship contract,
ii Develop a servicing activity schedule, and
iii Communicate the servicing plan with the sponsor.

Throughout these three steps, you have to always remind yourself about the specific preestablished objectives of the sponsor. Ultimately, regardless of the day-to-day challenges you face related to the sponsorship, your job is to enable the sponsor to achieve its objectives.

Each of the steps of the fulfillment of contractual commitments stage is described in the following sections.

Step 1: review the sponsorship contract

For any property, or the agency working on their behalf, the first step in servicing a sponsorship is to review the sponsorship contract in detail line-by-line. Then, based on the review, list each and every commitment within the contract and establish a plan for to deliver on each as the sponsor has asked. As you know by now, the list of sponsorship commitments will differ from one sponsorship to the next. For example, a multinational company that sponsors the FIFA World Cup will typically have a long list of commitments in the sponsorship contract, while the local coffee shop sponsor of a high-school soccer team will likely have fewer and less elaborate commitments to deliver on.

Although the list of commitments in each sponsorship contract will differ, there are a few common elements that are typically included in any sponsorship contract. These typically were also captured in the sponsorship package that the sponsor and property agreed to in the sales process. Specifically, the signed contract normally includes the elements of the agreed-to sponsorship package, plus some additional legal and logistical elements that are to be agreed to, such as:

- Full address of the sponsor, property, and any agency representation
- Description of the sponsored property (i.e., the assets the property is providing)
- Definition and interpretation (i.e., legal status of the entities involved)
- Grant of rights (i.e., what assets the parties grant to each other, typically the sponsorship package details)
- Use of the marks and rights (i.e., what each party is allowed in terms of the use of the brand, name, and logos of the other)
- Sponsorship fees (i.e., the amount to be paid to the property)
- Provision of marketing materials (i.e., what the sponsor will provide)
- Term and duration (i.e., the length of the agreement and terms for termination)
- Liabilities and insurance (i.e., responsibilities of each party is a problem occurs)

- Force majeure (i.e., what happens if something out of either party's control, such as a pandemic or inclement weather, impacts the sponsorship)
- Confidentiality
- Signatures

As noted, what is listed under the clause "grant of rights" usually, but not always, will be the sponsorship package, which includes the deliverables or commitments that you, the property, agreed to provide and that the sponsor expects from you. A sponsorship package can also be described as the agreed-on approach to the activation and servicing of the sponsorship that the two parties agree to execute together.

Some of the most common elements included in a sponsorship package (and the sponsorship contract) are as follows.

- *Placement of signage:* this includes banners, backdrops, logos on screens, logos on T-shirts or other equipment, logos on the billboards, web banners, social media sites, in-stadium screens, postevent interview backdrops, medal ribbons, and on-the-field logo prints. Normally, the specific number, size, location, and duration of the signage commitments will be specified.
- *Exclusivity:* a guarantee that the sponsor's competitors will not be allowed to become involved with the property in any form or on any platform. For example, if Pepsi is the official soft drink sponsor of a sport property, an exclusivity clause in the sponsorship package will provide the assurance to Pepsi that Coca-Cola, Dr. Pepper, or any other competitor will not be allowed any involvement in the event in any official capacity.
- *Right to use event trademarks and logos:* properties generally have terms and symbols that are legally protected. It is illegal to use such intellectual property without the permission of the owner. These are often called "pass-through rights", where the brand gives the property the right or the property gives the brant the right (or both) to use the trademarks and/or logos of the other party. For example, during the FIFA World Cup, it is common to see the FIFA logo and the trophy printed on Coca-Cola packaging and delivery vehicles.
- *Sponsorship level:* sponsorship levels include title sponsor (naming an event after the sponsor, e.g., TCS New York City Marathon), a presenting sponsor (e.g., TCS New York City Marathon presented

by New Balance), an association sponsor (a lower level after title and presenting), and a supporting/supplier sponsor (usually, in-kind sponsors). Levels vary considerably by sponsorship and can also be categorized according to tiers (tier 1, tier 2, and tier 3), or as platinum, gold, bronze, and silver levels. Some sport properties use a two-level system (e.g., Premium Partners and Partners) or something similar as well.

- *Distribution rights*: any rights to use a sport property as a distribution outlet, for example, for the sale of products or distribution of free samples at the event venue will also be outlined. For example, a bank sponsor may get the right to set up an ATM machine during a rugby tournament or a lottery corporation a spot to sell tickets.

- *Link on the event website*: allowing visitors to the event's website to click on an icon that will take them to the sponsor's website.

- *Social media cross-promotion*: the sponsor and property both commit to communicate the sponsorship official association with the property. The package will normally specify the number of posts and the timing.

- *Hospitality offerings*: Free tickets for sponsors' guests, access to VIP areas, refreshment services, and opportunities to meet athletes (or other celebrities). The package will normally specify the specifics of each offering.

Based on the contract and the package, a detailed commitments list can be developed. For example, under "placement of signage", the agreement lists the specific number, size, location, and duration of different signages such as banners, backdrops, billboards, web banners, in-stadium screens, interview backdrops, and medal ribbons. So you need to list them all down and plan the execution of each and every commitment, which is the second step in the sponsorship servicing process.

Step 2: develop a servicing activity schedule

With your list of deliverables from Step 1 in hand, you now need to develop what we refer to as a servicing activity path or schedule, which is a tool to help you to organize the commitments/deliverables, set timelines, assign human resources, and allocate budget. Most importantly, it helps you follow up and monitor the progress of the servicing activities you implement.

The servicing activity path includes the commitment task (by order) to be completed, the name of the person responsible for completing the task, and the date by which the task must be completed. These are widely accepted project management steps, but they need to be detailed, given their importance if the servicing is to take place. For example, you should not just put "banner" in the activity schedule; rather, the detailed activities before displaying the banner, such as the conception of the design of the banner, the design of the banner itself, the printing of the banner, the shipment and delivery of the banner, and the display of the banner must all be included with timelines and responsibility for each step noted since this process takes a certain period of time and involves a number of different people.

Your schedule tool can be created with any calendar software or spreadsheet software on your smartphone, tablet, laptop, or computer. You can also have a hard copy of it on in an old-fashioned written document, hard copy calendar, or book.

In order to help you construct your own schedule, we outline here a modified version of Anderson et al.'s (2018) nine-step approach to developing your servicing activities schedule:

1   Start with the identified detailed list of commitments from the contract (Step 1 above) and enter each as a servicing activity.
2   Determine the required presteps for each servicing activity.
3   Estimate the completion time required to delivery on each servicing activity.
4   Determine the time interval needed between #1 (a commitment – e.g., displaying a banner at a venue) and #2 (the presteps – e.g., designing, printing, shipping, and then displaying the banner).
5   Use the commitment delivery date and the prestep time estimates to determine the earliest start and earliest finish time for each servicing activity. The combination of the various delivery dates and timing can allow for an overall assessment of the total time required to finish the project.
6   Use the project completion time identified in step 5 as the latest finish time for the last activity and make a backward pass through the network to identify the latest start and latest finish for each activity.
7   Use the difference between the latest start time and the earliest start time for each activity and determine the slack (i.e., human resource availability) for each activity.
8   Use the information from steps 5 and 6 to finalize the overall activity schedule for the project.

As you develop timelines, you need to assign the responsible person for each task and determine the corresponding cost involved in undertaking each. Once, you have developed your servicing activity schedule, the next step is communicating the plan with the sponsor, which helps increase confidence in the relationship and build trust between the property and the sponsor that the sponsorship will be serviced as planned.

Step 3: communicate with the sponsor

With the list of commitments ready to share and a schedule in place to service each, it is time to engage the sponsor (or their agency) to align the plan with their preestablished sponsorship objectives. If it is a multi-year deal, review the previous year's efforts on servicing, and also identify the right contact person at the sponsor who will be responsible for servicing. The process has been sequential to this stage (steps 1 and 2) and now loops back and adjustments will be made taking the sponsor-side input into consideration.

Following a sponsor's input and a developed awareness of the importance, the risk, and the needs associated with the sponsorship, you may need to create at this stage what we refer to as a reinvestment framework. A reinvestment framework is an assessment of possible scenarios and allocating a proportion of the rights fees received back to servicing. For instance, a property reinvestment framework could be something like this:

- Level A – High Risk/High Value (i.e., sponsorship rights fees are important, renewal is at risk, and no replacement sponsor is in place, or a sponsorship with a strong chance for increased rights fees or an interested competing sponsor) – reinvest a significant amount of the rights fees (i.e., 5%–10%) in order to maximize the service efficiency and address any poorly serviced elements.
- Level B – Mid Value (i.e., a sponsorship of a lower rights few but where some concern about renewal or an observed opportunity for increased rights fees exists) – reinvest a modest amount (i.e., 1%–4%) to keep sponsor serviced and satisfied.
- Level C – Low Value (i.e., a sponsorship where the brand does very little or no activation and servicing investment/resources would not be warranted) – no reinvestment

Please note that, as a sport property, your communication with your sponsor regarding servicing should not be a one-off communication. It has to be an ongoing engagement. For example, if you are producing a piece of promotional material related to your property, you need to get the sponsor's approval on artwork and use of marks. Remember, sponsors may be sensitive or have legal restrictions when it comes to their image or use of their logo and marks. Showing attention to these details will demonstrate to your sponsor that you have responsible personnel to handle this and other similar undertakings.

Case study 4.1 A story of a well-serviced sponsorship – by the authors

As authors, we all have experience working with real-life sponsorships, in roles with brands, properties, and agencies. And, in these experiences, we have witnessed many well-serviced sponsorships and many that were left lacking. This is the story of a particularly well-serviced one, from which we think you can observe the type of "overservicing" approach that can be very successful within this tactic.

Due to confidentiality requirements, the names of the brand and the property are not disclosed.

It is the story of a medium-sized sport property and a sponsor in the financial services sector. It was a long-term partnership, that was up for renewal for the third time. However, in this case, the sponsor's objectives has shifted due to a rebrand and major changes to the environment for its core product.

The head of the sport property, however, was well versed in servicing and more than a year before the expiration of the deal, realizing it was in a high-risk situation (Level A from our framework earlier in the chapter) for nonrenewal with no likely replacement, she responded by immediately engaging her team and two external agencies to enhance the chance of renewal. This involved five key steps.

First, she ramped up her communications with the sponsor and their marketing team – increased emails, calls, meetings, updates, and social media shares.

Second, she engaged her marketing team to increase the number of shares, tags, links, and comments on the sponsor's social media channels via their channels.

Third, she provided enhanced opportunities – beyond what was in the existing sponsorship contract – for VIP experiences involving athletes and events, for the sponsor contacts.

Fourth, she engaged a creative agency to update their joint materials – involving the sponsor – including logos, social media creative, and more.

Finally, and most importantly, she learned – through the enhanced conversations – that the sponsor was now very interested in the awareness levels of their new brand and new products, replacing previous objectives related to hospitality and experiential activations. Thus, she hired a research agency to go back and assess the historical impact of the sponsorship on awareness (going back to the start of the partnership many years before), which showed very strong impact for the sponsor.

To conclude, the story ends well as the sponsorship was renewed, with the sponsor giving credit largely to the historical evaluation as the reason why they shifted from not planning to renew to renewal.

Sponsorship servicing: creating value-added activities

As noted in the case study on a successful sponsorship servicing effort, we would like to conclude this chapter with a section that emphasizes and provides insight into how to build and implement value-added servicing activities (such as the updated creative noted in the case study). These are items extend or add to the sponsorship commitments listed in the contract. On the one hand, they can include most of (if not all) the promotional opportunities available with your property but expanded to provide added value (e.g., enhanced support of existing items). On the other hand, it could be new servicing tactics such as the historical valuation noted in the case study.

The thinking behind "adding value" to the commitments on your list is that you will be able to overdeliver to your sponsor, improve the chances to renew the sponsorship and/or renegotiate the rights fee amount, motivate activation spend by the sponsor, and demonstrate the promotional potential of your property to other potential sponsors.

It is important to realize that there is often something unique and innovative that you could potentially be able to find to offer to a sponsor that is value added and that you can deliver on. It is imperative, from the sport property perspective, to only include elements that you can deliver on if you are hoping to have the sponsorship renewed in the future and, ideally, renewed at a higher rights fee level.

Yes, no one knows your property better than you do, and no one will be in a better position than you to come up with creative approaches to offer your sponsor. Looking at the different dimensions of your property and your audiences, you can come up with initiative(s) that can create added or extra value to a sponsor. For instance, digital media devices (including social media) are engaging, cost-effective, and easy to use, but their use to improve sponsorship servicing requires creativity, meaning that you are only limited by your imagination. In this regard, we particularly encourage properties to take advantage of social media and its unique features in reaching target audiences. As noted in Chapter 3, social media has the power of drawing more followers with similar needs to a platform and, by extension, aggregating reachable target audiences of a specific sport. Hence, communicating your sponsor's objectives via your social media platforms allows a sponsor to have a direct access to those who are responsive to its marketing communication efforts, which is an efficient and effective way to reach a target market.

Properties can also extend (as noted) initiatives from their existing servicing activities. For example, a 5K run may offer a weekend training program prior to the event day and offer a sponsor the opportunity to use the training sessions to reach those athletes with a service not committed to in the contract.

The fulfillment report

The final phase of sponsorship servicing is the report generated and provided to the sponsor. Often called a fulfillment report, it is a summarized progress report that outlines to sponsors what and how you delivered on the commitments you promised. It is important to differentiate here between a sponsorship evaluation and a fulfillment report. While sponsorship evaluation assesses the level of success of the sponsorship against preestablished sponsorship objectives, the fulfillment report is a document that summarizes the servicing activities undertaken by presenting information on the list of sponsorship commitments delivered by the property holder. In other words, while sponsorship evaluation is concerned with what a property has produced for the sponsor (e.g., creating awareness), the fulfillment report is concerned with how the property serviced the contract (e.g., producing banners) and the partnership order to enable the sponsor to achieve its objectives.

The fulfillment report captures the results of your servicing activity schedule (your plan). It is an evolving report that typically ends up being a comprehensive report of all the elements put in place to service the given sponsorship. Ultimately, and ideally, the final version is presented to the sponsor. However, some sponsors will also require regular updates monthly or quarterly of the fulfillment report. There may also be different versions of the report. For instance, your direct client (e.g., sponsorship manager) may want a very detailed report with all the items in your schedule, while they would prefer a higher-level executive summary style version for their boss (e.g., VP of marketing). Importantly, in a situation where your contact at the sponsor changes and a new person comes in, your fulfillment report can help get the new person on track and facilitate the building of a relationship on the account with her/him. The general purpose behind a fulfillment report is threefold, including (i) to monitor progress, (ii) to use it as a communication tool amongst your team, and (iii) to identify the tasks to be completed. Of primary importance, from the property perspective, is to ensure that the sponsor is aware that you delivered on all of the commitments that you promised.

Some may also use fulfillment reports as a postsponsorship report at debriefings. In these cases, the use of photos and videos alongside the written report is recommended. The content related to your achievements on sponsorship servicing may include the number of people who attended, the celebrities who attended, live media coverage, and social media coverage and interest. For example, the fulfillment report should include a summary of servicing activities, such as number of emails sent out, posters and flyers distributed, roller-up banners displayed, and doodie bags.

References

Anderson, D.R., Sweeney, D.J., Williams, T.A., Camm, J.D., & Cochran, J.J. (2018). *An introduction to management science: Quantitative approach.* Boston, MA: Cengage learning.

O'Reilly, N., & Huybers, T. (2015). Servicing in sponsorship: A best-worst scaling empirical analysis. *Journal of Sport Management, 29*(2), 153–169.

5   Sport sponsorship evaluation

Sponsorship evaluation

Imagine the following story.

As race director, you spent the last 12 months of your life organizing an adventure race, and the final participant of the race has just crossed the line. She is the 4,312th finisher of the 4,800 participants who started the adventure race almost 12 hours ago. They set out to complete more than 25 km of tough trails, filled with obstacles and challenges that your team spent the previous week building. Your team built the race course just as the sun rose on the first day and now, as the sun is setting, the cutoff time has arrived and your final finisher is recorded. By the feedback that you have received, people loved it and enjoyed the challenge. About 500 starters, however, did not make it. There were no major injuries and they left having given it their best shot or being bested by a nagging injury they had going in. Not a single negative complaint was received from your participants. On parking, aid stations, the course, the venue, directions in the woods, safety, and more, your team had performed well on all fronts. You had some challenges and had learned a lot in the previous years, and looking at this year's race, "it is about time" you thought to yourself, as this was the sixth annual version of your event.

Even though you had slept only a few hours in the past few days, the thought that this was year #6 immediately brought a thought, a scary one, into your tired brain. *Yikes*, you thought to yourself as you realized that your new title sponsor (the first one you have had in the six years of the event) has a three-year contract with you. But there is a clause in the agreement that states a renewal after the first year depends on an evaluation, which you had promised them in your contract. You quickly called your event manager asking if a plan was in place to evaluate the title sponsor's objectives. You received a reply: "No, but we have got

DOI: 10.4324/9781003154631-5

lots of photos and can download our social media analytics tomorrow to see how well we did."

This is the classic sponsorship evaluation problem, or really the challenge facing any performance measurement in the marketing communications industry. Yes, the event manager's answer is a part of sponsorship servicing and a fulfillment report. But, it is not a sponsorship evaluation!

And you might ask, what is that specific problem? Well, it is the fact that (i) evaluation is often done after the fact (i.e., postevent), (ii) it can be done with limited thought about the objectives of the sponsor, and (iii) it may be done with no planning into how to get data to inform research about the ability of the sponsorship to achieve those objectives.

A pundit might say, who cares! And they might add that you can always find evidence of success or something to share.

Certainly, a sport property – like our race director example above – could get lucky that social media reach or cool photos of their logo at the event were the goals of the sponsor. But, as you know from previous chapters in the book, this is unlikely to be the case given the size of investments, the volume of different objectives sought, and the intense competition that exists in the sport sponsorship marketplace. Further, this approach violates all of the three core rules of any sponsorship evaluation, which are as follows.

1   You need to *identify the objectives* up front, that is, to understand what the sponsor specifically wants to achieve with the sponsorship (e.g., to increase sales of a certain product).
2   You need to have a *benchmark* for each of those objectives. This means that you need to know where the sponsor is currently at so that you have something to compare against. For instance, a brand may know that their market share in a given region is 4.1%.
3   You need to have a *method* by which to measure each of the objectives to assess if the sponsorship has had any impact. For example, the brand may have an ongoing survey of customers to which a question can be added about the influence of the specific sponsorship on their past purchases and future purchase intention. On this point, it is worth noting that there are some objectives that can be measured in dollar value (e.g., onsite sales, new product orders, wholesale commitments), some other objectives can be measured in volume (e.g., visits to website, downloads, coupon redemptions, employee participation), and others require measurement by less precise scales or rankings, such as brand

image enhancement, showcasing community responsibility, employee satisfaction, and intent-to-purchase.

Thus, as this chapter will outline, a proactive, objectives-based approach to sponsorship evaluation is needed. And, as we will show, this does not necessarily require a massive investment of time or money, just some up-front collaborative planning and attention during the sponsorship. By collaborative we mean that there are some planning that has to take place before the commencement of the evaluation between the sponsor and the property.

The attribution issue

A major challenge in any evaluation is the notion of attribution, defined as the ability to determine if a certain consumer action can be traced back (i.e., attributed) to a particular marketing action. In fact, some industry people and academics claim that attribution means that sponsorship cannot be evaluated.

We wholeheartedly disagree.

Of course, sponsorship evaluation is not a perfect science, nor is any performance measurement for that matter. In reality, what we need is a good-enough analysis to make business decisions like, "Should we renew?" or "Are we charging enough?" or "Do we have the right activation mix?" In response, a well-planned sport sponsorship evaluation process can accomplish this for us – one where we can estimate the effect of a sponsorship on a decision to purchase a sponsor's brand by a targeted attendee of a sport property in comparison with other marketing tactics (advertising, public relations, sales promotions, etc.).

To illustrate further, let us say that the title sponsor of the adventure race that we started this chapter with is a national coffee brand and the event organizers were able to survey the participants post-race, asking about (i) their coffee preferences and (ii) if the sponsor's support of the event had influenced their purchase of the sponsor's coffee. The survey would have questions related to the title sponsor brand and all of its competitors, as well as all of its various marketing activities. Such questions help to estimate the influence (if any) of the sponsorship on changes (if any) of the purchase intentions of participants. Thus, although there would be a margin of error, the attribution of the sponsorship to intent-to-purchase in participants could be estimated and used to inform decision-making around renewal, pricing, activations, and other sponsorship elements.

AUTHORS' BLOG: EVALUATION IS NOT EXPENSIVE

So we want to put this out there in a very strong way.

There is a massive, even monstrous, misperception out there that sponsorship evaluation is expensive, time-consuming and requires people with master's degrees in analytics from highbrow universities.

Sure, if you are a leading premier league club in Europe or an NFL club in the United States with a global reach and nine-figure sponsorship revenues, you want world-class, vast, and highly reliable data done by the best agencies on the planet. We get that.

The reality, however, is that any sport property can do an evaluation, even without a budget (or just an extremely small one). If you follow the process outlined later in this chapter, you will know your sponsor's objectives and where they are currently at on that objective (i.e., benchmark). From there, you can consider how to capture some data to inform future decisions on that sponsorship. This could involve anything as simple as including a quick online survey to postevent participants with an incentive such as a draw for a free entry to the following year's event. You could also have a few volunteers or interns with iPads in the parking lots or use a free (or low-cost) social media analytics tool to track mentions or comments related to your sponsors. The options are numerous. The only requirement is that they focus on the sponsor's objectives. They are not perfect, but are they good enough to inform future decisions? Yes.

So, what are we trying to say?

Well, it is quite simple really. As you embark on a sport sponsorship journey, put evaluation at the same level as sales, activation, and servicing. If this was a family, all are children and should be treated equally. Having an evaluation – even a low-cost ad hoc one – will help all of its siblings a lot.

Sales is easier with evidence of success.

Activation choices can be better made (added, changed, removed, altered) with an understanding of what worked and what didn't.

Servicing can be assessed if we know what those we serviced think.

So there you have it. Make evaluation a priority.

Evaluation: the sponsor perspective

Our years of evaluating and studying sponsorship have shown us that when it is implemented effectively and in the appropriate fashion, sponsorship is well supported to be a promotional tactic of choice for brands to reach their target markets with a call-to-action. However, as sponsorship budgets increase and the cost to sponsor high-value sport properties continues to increase, the executives of brands are taking more and more interest in these choices due to their budget implications and their importance to the overall marketing communications efforts of their organizations. This includes increasing pressure on sponsorship managers to justify their sponsorship spending and be accountable for their sponsorship decisions.

Yes, the CMOs and CFOs of brands are taking more and more interest when they take on the role of sponsor of a sport property for hundreds of thousands and sometimes millions of dollars. Plus, they are investing that amount again – at least – in activation to leverage the rights fee spend they have made. This level of investment gets attention from the organization, and it demands that an ROI evaluation be done. Evaluations help sponsorship teams at the brand to be able to report back on what objectives were sought, how they were pursued (and why), and what the return was.

One of us authors was interviewing the CEO of a major Fortune 100 brand, who said that they would ask their sponsorship team to justify a sport sponsorship by answering the question, "Why don't we just lower the price of our products with the money we'd save by not spending on sponsorship?" The CEO, as the discussion went on, then informed that the poor answers to such questions led them to decide to not enter into some sponsorship deals and not renew some others. Clearly, the lack of evidence to support these investments led the CEO to decide to not use sponsorship.

There is a lesson here for sponsors, that a well-planned and properly implemented sponsorship with specific objectives (sales, image transfer, brand equity lift, etc.) that are evaluated in the right way (i.e., objectives, benchmarks, methods) is necessary to justify the use of sponsorship to senior management of brands. Indeed, we, and many others, know that sponsorship can work, but not always. And often it could work better, but the only way to determine this is undertake an evaluation.

There is published research (e.g., Abeza et al., 2020) to support that from the sponsor perspective, evaluation (i) serves as a guiding tool in making a strategic decision to invest in properties that deliver against the sponsor's objectives, (ii) enables sponsors to establish accountability for sponsorship for internal constituencies (e.g., the brand's Chief Financial Officer), (iii) assists with (re)negotiating rights fees and setting activation budgets, and (iv) provides the justification needed to secure and maintain sponsorships during challenging economic situations. Overall, evaluation enables sponsors to better appreciate the value of their sponsorship investment and articulate the possible rewards.

Misconceptions about sponsorship evaluation

The previous discussion might lead you to ask why sponsorships are not being evaluated as much as they should be.

Well, there are a few key reasons and we have lots of experience and research on this. Here's the list, and it is not long, as there are really five dominant reasons why sponsorships are not evaluated as often as they should be.

1   *Fear of a negative evaluation.* This is – by far – the main reason and it is observed in brands, properties, and agencies alike. Concerns around a result that shows that you picked the wrong partner or that the activation was off or that you should have done advertising are among the major subreasons. However, we argue that this is the wrong way to look at it. Quite simply, evidence that shows a misstep is a good thing, as it allows for learning to remedy the issue in the future. You know what to do next time, you know how to change, or you can communicate to your partners what went wrong with an action plan in place to fix it. The bottom line is that there is no need to be afraid.

2   *Low priority.* This reason is still there even as sponsorship matures in the sport industry. However, it is fortunately on the decline on the sponsor side as the cost of sport sponsorship rises. Most brands now have internal requirements to measure and justify significant marketing spends, including those on sponsorship. However, on the property side, there are still some instances where it is just not viewed as important or worth the cost of doing the evaluation. In these cases, there is often an assumption made that the brand will not care or that a deck of pictures (yes, we have seen that) is enough to make a sponsor sufficiently happy to renew a six-figure deal. If you work in the future for a property or for the agency representative of a property, make evaluation a priority.

3   *No data.* This is a challenging reason why that is typically based on either misconception of data availability or the reality that there is very limited data in that context. For instance, in certain niche sponsorship situations, such as the sponsorship of a sport property in equestrian, yachting, sailing, or modern pentathlon, where the brand is likely seeking to reach a very small but well-to-do target market via a sponsorship, access to data may be very limited or costly. Further, in these situations, the attribution issue may be more challenging, rendering the collection of relevant data more difficult. Give that we have all worked in these situations, we understand this one. However, we would point you to our authors blog earlier in this chapter and the sponsorship evaluation process (to follow) as a means to overcome this challenge. Particularly, we provide the insight how to find decent data at a reasonable cost.

In the case of the sponsor, much like the sponsor, the "no data" excuse to not evaluating is very shortsighted, we argue. And why do we say this? Well, if you do not have data to inform your activation and renewal decisions, as well as your negotiations on rights fees and contractual details, you are potentially wasting your marketing dollars, by either overspending on the sponsorships you have or missing out on the ones you should have (but don't because you do not have the data required to identify them).

4   *Assumption of value.* This is a minor reason (and may be a subset of #1 and fear of a negative result). It refers to the situation where a property (with a sponsor) believes that they have a level of value, which means that they do not need to gather or provide evidence to validate the value. In some cases, they try to "get by" with general info (e.g., TV ratings, website hits, number of attendees, media coverage) but without an evaluation specific to the sponsor objectives. In some cases, the assumption of value misconception is mitigated by the fact that the sponsor is doing its own evaluation of its own objectives. Thus, this may help with renewal, but it also might mean that the property may be undervaluing itself, as it has no evidence to negotiate with (while the sponsor does). In our experiences, in major sponsorships, each of the brand and the property has their own evaluations to inform the negotiations.

5   *Lack of expertise.* This is another common obstacle to evaluation that is on the decline due to a number of factors. These include (i) increasing numbers and quality of trained human resources grow (e.g., courses offered in sport management programs), (ii) a growing body of academic research on the topic area, and (iii) increasingly sophisticated industry practice around sponsorship

evaluation. However, in certain cases, some sponsors, properties, and agencies do not have the skills and background. This chapter can help you design your own evaluation.

To further drive home some of these points, one of us authors who has been an agency CEO for a quarter of a century has a very particular and experience-driven perspective that we, as a group, want to include from his point of view that outlines his journey with sponsorship evaluation and how much his view has changed over the years. See his advice in the following call-out box.

MARK HARRISON'S ADVICE: DON'T BE AFRAID OF THE TRUTH

I used to hate researchers. Hate them!

Given that I am writing this book with two researchers, I better clarify this inciteful comment in a hurry! My esteemed coauthors should take some immediate relief because this was a comment made in the past tense.

My mislaid dislike of researchers was rooted in one fundamentally flawed argument. Somehow, I thought I was smarter than the data – the data that researchers pursue, collect, analyze, and interpret daily from thousands and thousands of people.

Imagine the enormity of my ego. Not only did I think I was smarter than the several eccentric researchers that our clients worked with those days. (Sorry researchers, did I make fun of you again?) But somehow, I thought I was smarter than thousands of consumers!

Do you know who is smarter than thousands of consumers? The inventors Betamax, New Coke, and Meerkat. If you don't remember those three brands, here is the category they belong to – abject failure!

So, what changed in my head to realize that my ignorance of data was ill-fated? Simply put, it was getting in the room with the right type of researchers. The great researchers went beyond numbers and cells and data points.

The turning point for me was when I worked with a firm called IMI International. This team of global researchers truly understood the critical success factors in sponsorship and what

---

contributed to a successful campaign and what did not. Over time, I also got exposed to other firms such as Ipsos, Repucom (later bought by Nielsen), Block Six Analytics, and MVPindex. These firms bring varied and new approaches to understand the impact of sponsorship programs, consumer engagement, and marketing effectiveness.

If I was to dig a little deeper, my change in approach was also influenced by working with my coauthor, Norm O'Reilly, and seeing the impact of his methods on our clients. Suddenly, my bravado, street smarts, and chutzpah to pitch my ideas were reinforced by intel, insight, and information. The clients suddenly had an entirely different reaction to our presentations – not only our clients but also our team. The utilization of excellent research, guided by a great researcher's hands, is akin to knowing an opposing football team's playbook. You feel like you understand the secret codices and have signals to intercept any possible client objection to a recommendation in a meeting.

As my conversion from hater to fanboy evolved over the years, my devotion to the craft of valuation and evaluation only grew larger. Now my drumbeats were impossible to ignore as I orchestrated campaign after campaign and insisted that our staff, our partners, and our clients all admit to researching.

Now, it would be a great crescendo to metaphor to inform you that doing an evaluation always works. That every time we recommend evaluation work, our client's buy-in and success follows. But that would be a lie. You can mark an X down on your research scorecard for that. It is a very frustrating bone of contention for many of us in this industry.

Perhaps you want to take a stab at this question. Why in the world would any client, brand, agency, or property want to resist research? It is straightforward. They are afraid of the Truth!

Yes, it is true. I said it. I just accused my entire industry of subconscious fraud. We like to parade around talking about how powerful, impactful, and memorable sponsorship marketing can be. But when some industry players get asked, they sing, dance, run, and hide.

Don't be afraid of the Truth!

I mean, what is there to be afraid of, my friends?

It is perhaps losing the account if you are an agency.

Or you are losing the sponsorship if you are a property.

There could be a threat to your promotability if you are the sponsor.

There could be concerns over lost commissions if you are a salesperson.

But does the Truth hurt? Wouldn't knowing the Truth and knowing it early on improve your programs? How can you suggest that not evaluating significant allocations of resources, cash, and time to understand your progress would be an impediment? Am I the only one in the room who thinks that listening to consumers, key influencers, and experts would be worthwhile? That is, tweaking our campaigns to generate more engagement and impact would be responsible.

If you are afraid of the Truth, you will lose more than your commission or your contract. You will lose the trust of your sponsor. Once you have lost that trust, it is the hardest thing to rebuild.

Allow me to repeat and expand on that point. Losing someone's faith is a long-lasting injury to your reputation and career. You can make a mistake and recover. You can have an omission and apologize. You can be late with delivery and rush it to the finish line. But there are no Band-Aids, crutches, or tablets to restore a breach of trust.

However, if you have enough confidence in what you are doing to bring in the experts and the third-party validators and work with them to assess your work, you will build a lifetime supply of trust with all of your partners. Trust me, from a trust position, you are that much more well suited to excel in your career. This truism applies to all stakeholders in sponsorship marketing.

No matter where you sit in the ecosystem, you need to partner with the truth-sayers – the fact-finders. The men and women represent the consumer's voice, the interpreters of the media impact, and the analysts of financial outcomes. Find yourself a research superhero today and enjoy a long-lasting career of real success.

Did I mention I love researchers?

Mark's advice is clear and vitally important to anyone working in sponsorship. One can overcome the obstacles to evaluation without vast resources. You can evaluate your sponsorship in an effective way and improve not only your own sponsorships but the practice overall.

Let us give you an example. The case study that follows outlines the move of a major global brand to end a sponsorship of a set of sport properties that – based on our read of the public data – is likely based on an evaluation, or a series of evaluations.

Case study 5.1 AIG leaves the All Blacks and Black Ferns[1]

It is rare that the termination of a sponsorship contract receives more attention than the signing of a new sponsor, but when a large American firm leaves the most successful rugby program in the sport's history, that makes headlines. Clearly, evaluations of the sponsorship's effectiveness for AIG have not led to sufficient results for AIG to renew. So, after more than a decade of this sponsorship, the insurance firm AIG will end its partnership with the New Zealand All Blacks at the end of 2021. In 2012, AIG signed a five-year deal reportedly worth USD$80 million, and in 2016 signed a USD$10–20 million per year six-year extension. The later deal includes sponsorship of not only the New Zealand senior men's national team – the All Blacks – but also the All Blacks Sevens, the Maori All Blacks, the Black Ferns, the New Zealand Black Ferns Sevens, and the New Zealand U-20 teams.

"Through this partnership, New Zealand Rugby [NZR] and the six national teams sponsored by AIG have been able to grow rugby's presence in new and growing markets, with opportunities to play in new territories and introduce our teams to new fans all over the world", said Mark Robinson, NZR CEO. Examples of AIG supporting the All Blacks and Black Ferns international rugby global reach included the All Blacks first-ever test match in the United States; triple header matches also featuring the Maori All Blacks, and Black Ferns in Chicago; the Maori All Blacks playing across Canada, Osaka, and Tokyo; and a tour of South America.

The deal has also seen numerous social media campaigns such as #EffortIsEffort and #DiversityIsStrength, promoting positive social messages and equality on and off the sporting field. These media campaigns have received international recognition, including the Clio Awards in New York. Clio Award is an annual award program that recognizes innovation and creative excellence in advertising, design, and communication.

On AIG's website, they cite the traits of teamwork, integrity, and performing at the highest level as shared characteristics of the All Blacks and AIG. However, reports also bring AIG's character into question as they decided to ensure the controversial Carmichael coal mine in Central Queensland, which antimining activists cited when calling for NZR to drop the insurance company as a sponsor in September 2019. AIG cites the need for more financial flexibility in its sporting sponsorships as a reason for leaving the All Blacks, providing the NZR with over a year's notice that the deal would not be renewed. This time frame was recognized by both parties as ample time to evaluate the corporate sponsorship landscape and provide the All Blacks with adequate time to find a new major sponsor.

Sponsorship evaluation: how do you do it?

Now, it is time to give you the tools that you need to perform a sponsorship evaluation. Before you start, it is very important that you realize that sponsorship evaluation is a process. And by a process we mean something where there is no easy formula or no "silver bullet" that you can easily employ to evaluate each and every sponsorship. We apologize in advance, but you will need to customize – at least to some extent – each and every sponsorship evaluation that you do, as methods and metrics will vary with each sponsorship objective, each activation, and each servicing activity.

Presented as Figure 5.1, we draw from our own process model (O'Reilly & Madill, 2012). This model has been widely used and adapted to other contexts, including health-focused sponsorship (Bagramian et al., 2019) and social marketing sponsorship (Madill et al., 2014).

So, how do you use the process? First, it is a stepwise approach grounded in a few important decisions to be made before even embarking on the evaluation.

Step #1 of the process model is setting the stage, which involves:

1   *Determining if a sport sponsorship evaluation is worth evaluating.*
    Ask yourself if the sponsorship is important enough and sizeable enough and if the sponsor has clearly defined objectives. If the answer is no to these questions, it might not be worth it.
2   *Assessing if the sponsorship is actually a sponsorship.* As noted in Chapters 1 and 2, sponsorship has its roots in philanthropy and, although rare, these sponsorships still exist, where the rationale is

CEO/owner interest and not potential marketing benefits. In these cases, an evaluation would not be recommended.

3 *Assessing if the cost-benefit make sense.* To answer this question, you need to do an initial assessment of the methods needed to acquire the data needed for a decision-informing evaluation and determine if it is worthwhile. For instance, if your review suggests that you likely need a survey of a large market by a market research agency, that will cost at least $15,000 for a sponsorship valued at $25,000, the cost-benefit would suggest that it is not worth proceeding.

4 *Being certain the sponsor(s) has(have) marketing objectives for the sponsorship.* This can be gleaned from the contract and conversations to know that the sponsors have objectives that are SMART (specific, measurable, achievable, results oriented, and time-bound), with benchmarks.

If these questions are all answered in a way that supports an evaluation, the remaining steps of the process will be followed per Figure 5.1.

Steps #2 and #3 are about identifying (#2) and articulating (#3) the objectives that the sponsor(s) has (have) in mind to accomplish from the sponsorship. The identification of the objectives is normally done via formal review of the contract, formal review of sponsor marketing materials, informal conversations with the sponsor(s), and informal discussions with the agency partners of the sponsor(s). A key element here is that the objectives of the property and any other intermediaries – including other sponsors (i.e., co-sponsors), agencies, and media partners – are also included here.

SPONSORSHIP EVALUATION - PROCESS MODEL

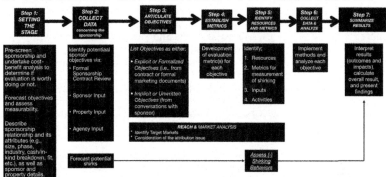

Figure 5.1 Sponsorship Evaluation Process Model.
Source: Adapted from O'Reilly and Madill (2012).

Pinpointing the objectives ensures that sponsorship is measured against clearly defined objectives (ROO) that are agreed on prior to the commencement of the evaluation. The objectives should be SMART in order to articulate the objectives that the evaluation is designed to measure. Per the process model, sponsors will be expected to clearly state the expectations that they have for their sponsorship investment. Importantly, when we say that "identifying objectives helps measurement", we do not refer to vague statements such as "increasing customers in a given market segment"; rather, they should be specifically written, such as "to increase consumers by 5,000" or "to raise market share by 1%".

The work involved in Steps #2 and #3 also includes efforts to identify any actions taken by any of the stakeholders that could undermine the impact of the sponsorship. In the model, these are known as "shirks" or "shirking behaviors", which are actions that undermine the sponsorship. This could include items like ambush marketing by a competitor of a sponsor that the property was not aware of, or poor sponsorship servicing efforts by the property with respect to the deliverable promised in the sponsorship contract.

To illustrate these steps, let us assume, as Abeza et al. (2020) discussed, that a car manufacturer is sponsoring a triathlon event. In this case, the sponsor wants to achieve the seven key objectives listed in Table 5.1. We provide examples of sample approaches that a property could offer toward achieving these objectives, which, in turn, guide the identification of measurement metrics discussed in step #4 of the process model.

Table 5.1 Sample Approaches to Achieve Sponsorship Objectives of a Car Manufacturer

Objectives	Executing Objectives (Sample Approaches)
Increase brand awareness	Signage and banners on the racecourse
Increase brand preference	Meet and greets and autograph sessions with high-profile athletes at the event sites
Lead generation	On-site activation through rebates, showcase new brand vehicles
Increase employee morale	Employees at local car dealer offices to be provided with an opportunity to participate
Reward existing customers	Premier parking and access to a hospitality tent
Brand engagement	Test drives
Reach new audiences	Contests that encourage users to upload images and videos on social media and prizes for the winners

Source: Adapted from Abeza et al. (2020).

Step #4 is perhaps the most important step in the process, where for each of the objectives specified and articulated in Step #3, as well as the possible shirks, a metric is determined with both a benchmark and a method to measure the impact of the sponsorship on that benchmark. This normally leads to a table or a spreadsheet with the list of objectives and shirks with an associated benchmark and method to measure each. To illustrate, a relatively straightforward example is provided below.

Table 5.2 is just a sample. There are a number of objectives sought by sponsors; therefore, you need to be prepared to develop benchmarks and metrics specific to each possible objective.

As noted in the figure representation of the process model, concurrent to Steps #3, #4, and #5, the identification of target markets needs to be undertaken. This involves identifying both the target markets

Table 5.2 Method to Measure Return on Objectives

Sponsor Objective	Benchmark	Method to Measure Return on Objectives
Increase market share in region	22% (current market share)	Tracking of market share (industry level data) with survey of new customers to assess attribution to sponsorship
Increase brand awareness in country	76% (current unaided recall)	National survey (unaided) of a representative sample to assess unaided recall in the country's population
Increase annual spend of top 1% of clients	$56,500 (top 1% average)	Internal (sponsor) tracking of top 1% plus survey of a sample of these clients to assess attribution of sponsorship
Achieve onsite sales of sponsor's product	15,000 units (based on forecast)	Sales tracking by sponsor
Potential shirk	Possible negative impact on the sought objective	Method to assess impact
Failure to deliver celebrity athlete appearance	VIP customer satisfaction and sales	Survey VIP customers to assess impact
Sponsor's competitor has presence at event	Ambush marketing	Survey participants and spectators to assess levels of confusion in identifying sponsor

of the sponsor(s), as well as the reach of the property. This goes back to the example from Chapter 4, where a multinational company that sponsors the FIFA World Cup will have a long list of commitments attached to its sponsorship contract and a wider global reach, as compared to a local coffee shop sponsoring a high school soccer team which will typically have a very short list of commitments and a much smaller geographical reach. The sponsorship objectives therefore need to be further divided by reach. For example, assume that the "increase annual spend of top 1% of clients" objective in Table 5.3 was for a sponsorship in Australia, where the target market analysis identified that the top 1% for this sponsor were divided between the cities of Sydney, Melbourne, and Canberra, with the target market in each of those cities having different characteristics. Thus, the single objective would become three, as follows.

Step #5 is the key step from a budgeting and data acquisition perspective, as it involves selecting the appropriate method for each of the identified objectives and shirks to be able to assess their impact. This is done pre-sponsorship and involves consideration of budget, options, and quality of data. For instance, for the top 1% example in Table 5.3 with the three markets, the evaluation could be done by a third-party agency who would do the interview and report back (high cost), or some staff time could be allocated from the sponsor's research team (medium cost, mostly the time of staff) or an intern could be hired (low cost).

Step #6 is the process of running the data collection and doing the analysis. As we mentioned earlier, there is no "silver bullet" way of evaluating a sponsorship. Indeed, as brands seek different objectives

Table 5.3 Illustration of a Method to Measure Return on Objectives

Sponsor Objective	Benchmark	Method to Measure Return on Objectives
Increase annual spend of top 1% of clients – Sydney	$86,200 (top 1% average in Sydney)	Internal (sponsor) tracking of top 1% plus survey of a sample of these clients to assess attribution of sponsorship with sampling of representative groups of respondents done in each of (i) Sydney, (ii) Melbourne, and (iii) Canberra.
Increase annual spend of top 1% of clients – Melbourne	$61,900 (top 1% average in Melbourne)	
Increase annual spend of top 1% of clients – Canberra	$47,100 (top 1% average in Canberra)	

from their sponsorships, different forms of data type, metrics, data collection instruments, and analytical approaches will be required for each sponsorship and each sponsorship objective. Step #7 is summarizing and linking the results back to the benchmarks and making an assessment of the overall effectiveness of the sponsorship by objective. Typically, Step #7 will list the benchmark, the outcome of the research, the impact of that outcome on the benchmark, and an assessment of the return of the sponsorship on that objective ("achieved", "low impact", etc.).

Sponsorship valuation is NOT sponsorship evaluation

As it is a topic of confusion for many practitioners, we wanted to add a short point of clarification for you. There is another area of sponsorship (that we have touched on earlier in the book) that should not be confused with sponsorship evaluation, that is, sponsorship valuation. The distinction is very important to anyone working in sponsorship and also helps clarify the role of sponsorship evaluation. Let us explain.

Undertaken by both sponsors and properties (or their agency representatives), sponsorship valuation (and not evaluation) involves estimating the value of a sponsorship, or what sponsors will be willing to pay for your property as part of a potential sponsorship, based on the assets that it includes (media reach, hospitality opportunities, sales opportunities, signage, social media content, etc.) at the level it is at (i.e., title, premium partner, etc.). A valuation is typically done prior to a sponsorship contract, and often in the prospecting stage, where a property is seeking to figure out what it might be worth for an interested brand or the brand is trying to determine what it should pay for a given property. In either case, the parties are seeking a valuation to inform their upcoming negotiations about the particular sponsorship.

For example, the NHL added helmet logos as a sponsorship opportunity for the 2020–2021 season (during the COVID-19 pandemic), thereby allowing NHL clubs to offer this additional asset to sponsors and potential sponsors. In this situation, a sponsorship valuation would involve an NHL club undertaking a sponsorship valuation to determine what the new asset might be worth or a potential sponsor doing their own valuation to assess, from their perspective, what it might be worth. In extending this example, the sponsorship evaluation (and not valuation) in the helmet sponsorship example could be an assessment of the helmet sponsorship by United Wholesale Mortgage of the Detroit Red Wings in the NHL. Here, the evaluation would be specific to the objectives of United Wholesale Mortgage and the impact of the sponsorship on those objectives. Although these objectives are not publicly shared, one could assume one would be to increase the number of mortgages sold, which could be measured via a fan survey or internal data base review by the mortgage company coupled with a survey of new customers.

There are three key considerations when doing a sponsorship valuation.

1   Revenue and expenses: On the sponsor side, will the sponsorship provide a return that is greater than the costs (rights fee plus activation costs)? On the property side, will the revenue provide a source of income sufficient to cover costs and contribute to the organization's goals?
2   Interested competitors. How many companies in the industry of the sponsor are interested in the particular sport property? This will have a significant impact on the valuation, as multiple interested competitors (e.g., Coke and Pepsi) will increase the valuation.
3   Organizational objectives. Is the property interested to aligning with certain selected brands or categories of brands? Are you more interested in keeping your existing sponsors and securing stability?

Summary

To conclude this chapter, we include a summary of about the comments of five sponsorship industry experts on sponsorship evaluation. These expert insights were generated from a SponsorshipX Clubhouse Panel that took place in Spring of 2021, that one of us authors moderated. The particular session was on the topic of measurement in sponsorship and it included six leading experts from around the world.

At the end of the session, we asked those experts to provide their tips to listeners, which we summarize as follows.

1   Brands should focus on those targets who like the property (e.g., fans) already in their efforts.
2   Properties should do a proper fan segmentation, including those who are not fans.
3   Brands need to own the evaluation and engage an independent third party to measure based on their objectives.
4   Properties and agencies need to understand the business priorities of the sponsor that they are trying to partner with and determine if sponsorship is the right approach to use for that sponsor.

5   Determine how the CMO of the sponsor is viewing the sponsorship (i.e., "their lens"), whether it is data, sales, brand, images, or another objective.

6   Properties need to take the time to understand their partner's objectives and do everything they can to support those efforts.

7   Media is not the answer to sponsorship measurement.

8   Lift (i.e., sales) for sponsors needs to be a core metric.

The experts included Indivar Kushari, COO of Q.i. Value Systems Inc.; Matthew Leopold, head of brand, PR, and content marketing at LexisNexis; Francois Robert, executive director of partnerships at the Canadian Paralympic Committee; Liz Rose, account director at The T1 Agency; Ian Thompson, independent sponsorship expert; and Kevin Wittner, vice-president at Octagon.

Note

1   https://www.sportbusiness.com/news/aig-opts-out-of-all-blacks-sponsorship-renewal/; https://www.rugbypass.com/news/new-zealand-rugbys-ground breaking-partnership-with-aig-comes-to-an-end/; https://insidersport.com/2020/01/14/aig-confirms-all-blacks-sponsorship-to-end-in-2021/; https://www.stuff.co.nz/business/118768679/all-blacks-on-the-market-for-new-major-sponsor-after-insurer-aig-calls-time; https://bit.ly/3cW6Kfa; https://bit.ly/2RcGNj0

References

Abeza, G., Seguin, B., Carton, P., & Holland, S. (2020). Measuring sponsorship effectiveness: Designing an alternative approach. *Sport Marketing Quarterly*. doi:10.32731/SMQ.OA.092020.01

Bagramian, R., Madill, J., O'Reilly, N., Deshpande, S., Rhodes, R.E., Tremblay, M., Berry, T., & Faulkner, G. (2019). Evaluation of sport participation objectives within a health-focused social marketing sponsorship. *International Journal of Sports Marketing & Sponsorship*, *20*(2), 206–223.

Madill, J., O'Reilly, N., & Nadeau, J. (2014). Financing social marketing programs through sponsorship: Implications for evaluation. *Journal of Social Marketing*, *4*(1), 22–37.

O'Reilly, N., & Madill, J. (2012). The development of a process for evaluating marketing sponsorships. *Canadian Journal of Administrative Sciences*, *29*(1), 50–66.

6 The future of sport sponsorship

Lessons, implications, and predictions for the future of sponsorship

This chapter is organized as a set of our observations, experiences, learning, and points drawn from the previous chapters. Based on these, we structure the insights that we want to share with you about the future of sport sponsorship, in the context of the sport industry, taking into consideration the current reality. The objective is to provide you with direction via a set of insights into sponsorship's future.

Insight #1: two past flaws of sponsorship need to be rectified

There are two "past flaws" that we have observed in many sport sponsorships. These are based on sponsorship professionals mistaking sponsorship for what it is not. There are two specific ones that we would like to highlight.

1 Hosting is not sponsorship.
2 Signage is not sponsorship.

Let us start with hosting. In many sponsorships in the past, in our experiences, the primary interest of the sponsor was to have hosting opportunities to attend (with tickets and accreditation). We observed this mainly at major events: professional sport games, world championship tournaments, Olympic/Paralympic Games, and similar events. The goal was networking, business development, entertainment, and personal brand building, all of which are good things for business and sponsorship outcomes alike. However, and this is our point here, they should not be the only and primary focus on engaging in a sponsorship.

DOI: 10.4324/9781003154631-6

These are activation tactics that should be used around a set of sponsorship objectives and a strategically developed set of tactics which likely include hosting.

Signage is used in a similar manner in many of the past sponsorships that we have been involved with. Whether digital or traditional, signs are often the focus of a sponsorship deal. However, the objectives that brands seek to achieve with sponsorship are much more than exposure. Additional objectives (knowledge, liking, image transfer, sales, etc.) often come after exposure or awareness has been established, and are illustrative of the misconception of considering signage as sponsorship. Although there are cases where a sponsor's objective is awareness creation, it is rare that a sponsor invests in sponsorship just for exposure since it a multifaceted marketing tool with many other advantages.

Insight #2: activate internally

Internal activation refers to the "power" of the employees of a brand as part of an activation. Thus, engaging salespeople, administrators, accountants, drivers, and all employees in a sponsorship could be one of the most effective ways of activation.

Why? The research shows that, due to their personal connection to the brand as their employer, if they feel engaged in the sponsorship and involved in it, they can serve as spokesperson and will better communicate it passionately externally. A research indicated that "content shared by an employee receives eight times more engagement than content shared by the brand, and that [sales] leads developed by employee social media communications converts 7 times more frequently than other [sales] leads" (Cornwell, 2021).

Thus, ask yourself on any sponsorship, *Are the employees of the brand engaged? Are they involved? Can we engage them more? Do they feel pride in the sponsorship? Are they informed about the property and its details?*

Insight #3: get data, no matter what

Data science (and its importance) is emerging as one of the key aspects of today's sport business. Reluctance around data usage in sponsorship evaluation may have resulted from a number of operational misconceptions such as a desire for the easy way, a fear (as you saw in Chapter 5) of a negative result, lack of understanding of analytics tools, and a failure to invest up front in setting benchmarks.

Particularly, there is a massive amount of digital data available today on consumers and the markets that sponsors seek to reach, but the key question is, "How is a brand going to use that massive data?" Well, drawing useful data from massive data set to produce meaningful insights is the key. This requires skilled and trained analysts to interpret and assess how it may be useful. Although they are expensive, the need to embrace data and engage skilled personnel is essential to make smarter decisions and optimize sponsorship.

In the case of sponsorship, it already has digital data, and will be increasingly so as time goes on. Be ready for it. How? Let us blog about it!

AUTHORS' BLOG: DATA BEFORE YOU MARRY

The future of sponsorship, especially in sports, is inextricably tied to the involvement of in-person spectators, participants, volunteers, and staff.

It has been said countless times during the COVID-19 pandemic that *Sport is Not Sport, Without Fans.* Superstar athletes such as LeBron James proclaimed in March 2020 that they would not play games without fans at the onset of the pandemic in North America. He changed his mind, played in a bubble, and took home a Larry O'B (the NBA Championship Trophy).

James was not wrong. Sports are not sports when played in a fanless bubble. Athletes do not get motivated by empty seats and streaming delayed spectators, and children are not engaged when playing by themselves. We have never met a high-performing athlete who can perfect their craft by conducting their training and coaching through video streaming.

All of us shudder to think of a future without fans.

Sponsors around the world would join us in that foreboding. Sport does not work without real-life fans. Now you might argue that makes no sense. Only a small percentage of fans ever get to go to a major league event due to cost, proximity, access, and scarcity. But the in-stadium fans are only a small percentage of the live fans that engage with sporting events. There are many other live fan situations.

Some people go to bars, pubs, and taverns to cheer on their teams. Some people go to friends', relatives', and neighbors' to enjoy the game. Some people tailgate and do not walk through the ticket wickets. Many people travel to the host city of significant multisport or multiday events and never set foot into the stadium or arena on a grander scale. The NCAA Men's Final Four, F1 races, and the Olympics are perfect examples of this phenomenon. Super Bowl weekend is the year's busiest in Las Vegas, despite its never hosting the game. Though that may sound odd, people want to be as close as possible to significant events – proximity matters.

The pandemic has destroyed all forms and levels of live engagement, as spectators are limited to small groups in their own homes. We have lost the energy created by fans gathering together and sharing their power.

This matters to sponsorship. It has left brands and properties with only their core fans to engage with, and it has destroyed the opportunity to bring new fans into the brand. Recently, the tools to amplify for sponsorship marketers were restricted to manicured digital and social executions.

Thankfully, it appears that vaccines will provide the needed wall of defense to allow live fans to engage with sports again. The savvy sponsorship practitioners will realize that this reprieve also opens the door to opportunity. That opportunity is to build more robust and sophisticated fan engagement tools. It is time for sponsorship to move beyond the T-shirt toss.

The easy-start is that every sponsorship property and all sponsors need to engage in a proper CRM (customer relationship management) strategy. They both need to focus on the single fan and understand their every behavior, action, impulse, need, and emotion. Sponsorship practitioners need to know when a fan is in the stadium, when they are at home, when they are on an e-commerce site, and when they are not interested in engaging with their team.

No one in the world does this. Yet every marketer knows that we are already waist-deep into the era of data. Data rules. Direct-to-consumer brands understand this, and brands such as Peloton have mastered this. Fintech marketers, network file transfer developers, and cryptocurrency markets are taking advantage of this.

As sponsorship marketers, we have no choice. There will be no future for our business if we do not fully embrace understanding the customer. Being a part of their journey in an additive and progressive manner is essential for our marketing purposes and the customer's benefit. If sponsorships do not embrace this, their role in the business equation will be diminished and eventually replaced.

The business entity that can best provide omnichannel connection to customers will receive the mandate to lead. Think of organizations like Fanatics that do a brilliant job of tailoring their offerings based on your team's results. Imagine if they, and other merchandisers, take the CRM lead. Brands will not do sponsorships. They will do licensing deals with merchandisers and effectively provide companies and brands with digital shelf space to leverage to market to purchasers.

If all of this feels far-fetched to you, think about the newspaper business. When your parents were young, the paper came to them, usually at home, but often to the office. The paper publishers had some simple metrics on readership and none on engagement. Now think about how you consume media. It travels with you. It streams on several devices that you own. It can be paused, delayed, recorded, reread, rewound, and repeated.

Now, which entity knows more about you?

If you are a brand, would you want to advertise in a newspaper or create a promotional activity with a digital partner?

Yes, we know that comparisons to newspapers are overstating the obvious. But that is the difference between sponsorship today and where it needs to go to survive.

Insight #4: embrace the COVID-19 accelerants

Again, we will draw from recent research to support an insight. There was a research that we led during the pandemic, namely, the series of SponsorshipX COVID impact studies (SponsorshipX, 2020), which collected data on four occasions during the pandemic – in the spring, early summer, late summer, and fall of 2020, when much certainty in the marketplace existed. These studies, which were based on the input of sponsorship industry professionals from around the world, provided insights on a few key findings that were accelerated by COVID-19 and that will last well beyond COVID-19. Thus, the pandemic can be viewed as an accelerant.

Here are five points that we picked up on.

1   *Be authentic.* We learned that, as brands, if you plan to sponsor or activate around COVID-19, such as leveraging the front-line workers in the pandemic, you should only do so if it makes sense with your brand, fits with your marketing, and will not be viewed by consumers as taking advantage of the situation. In other words, be very cautious around a pivot related to the pandemic. If you are viewed as taking advantage, your brand will be negatively impacted. Comments from industry professionals included "avoid choosing a theme of the season", "do not try to be clever", and "only pivot if it makes sense long term".

2   *Hybrid is the new standard.* Many properties and sponsor activations went digital in the 2020–2021 period. Many are expecting to go back to a traditional, live events–based world. We are saying that this is not the case for most. The new reality, where the new standard or baseline will be, is the hybrid sport property. By hybrid this refers to both in-person and media-linked involvement of spectators, fans, and participants alike in any sport property, in a post-COVID world. Examples include virtual exhibitions, hybrid events, sport bubbles, live viewing experiences, and interactive festivals.

3   *Mental health is a sponsorship asset.* Certainly, mental health has been important in cause-related marketing efforts in the past, but the pandemic brought its severity, common occurrence, and relevance to all to the mainstream. In turn, it has become a cause that many brands value, and therefore a potential sponsorship asset for sport properties and their agencies. Further, the pandemic, in many countries, has highlighted the role of sport participation and physical activity in both the physical and mental health of populations. This is an area of importance for sponsorship investment and activation, we argue.

4   *Food insecurity is a sponsorship asset.* Similar to mental health, the early stages of the pandemic emphasized the importance of food, access to food, and the availability of safe food to many. Many food manufacturers picked up on this, making it a new sponsorship category.

5   *Pausing, planning, and investing can be a smart move.* A very common insight provided by the respondents to the surveys was that those properties that were small, lacked digital capacity, required live events, and did not have an authentic way to change should stop, strategize, and build.

Insight #5: cryptocurrency is getting into sponsorship

A form of digital cash or virtual money, cryptocurrency is an electronic currency system that uses disturbed ledger technology (blockchain) that is fully digital and has no central authority (e.g., country). Initially conceived in the early 1980s, and first brought to the market in 2009 (bitcoin), it continues to attract attention in an increasingly virtual world. Although it is, at this stage, something to just keep your eye on, there is evidence of growth. In March 2021, there are two new examples of cryptocurrency sponsorships. The first is the naming rights deal for FTX Arena (in Miami-Dade Florida) where the Miami Heat of the NBA play. FTX is a cryptocurrency exchange. The second is the sponsorship by another cryptocurrency exchange, crypto.com, of the NHL's Montreal Canadiens.

Insight #6: esports is rising

Esports burst upon the scene over the past decade and has sustained during COVID-19 when so many other sport properties did not. One prevailing notion about esports that we encourage everyone in our industry to move on from is the view the esports is not sport, that it is somehow external to the field.

There is considerable evidence of the ability of esports to support brands, including nonendemic ones, with their marketing goals, as noted in the case study below about esports' most popular athlete and most used platform. Endemic sponsors are those brands closely affiliated with esport (i.e., based in the esports industry) and nonendemic (i.e., a nonesports brand marketing through esports with sponsorship). Examples of endemic sponsors include software companies (e.g., Microsoft) and hardware brands (e.g., Intel, Sony). The nonendemic sponsors include energy drink companies (e.g., Mountain Dew, Red Bull, Monster), car manufacturers (e.g., Audi, Mercedes-Benz), and fast-food companies (e.g., McDonald's).

Case study 6.1 Esports, Twitch, Ninja, and non-endemic sponsorships[1]

Twitch is the top video game streaming platform, one that many brands have sought to leverage for marketing purposes, including sponsorship. In recent years, many nonendemic brands looking to reach the loyal followers of Twitch streamers has increased. In December 2020, esports legend Tyler Blevins, commonly known as Ninja, was the most followed Twitch channel, with an estimated 17 million followers and an estimated net worth of USD$25 million. Here are a few examples of nonendemic sponsorships involving Twitch and Ninja.

1 Leading up to TwitchCon 2018, Ninja collaborated with fellow Twitch streamer DrLupo to promote Hershey's Reese's Pieces mashup bar. The activation featured a 12-hour livestream including infrequent mentioning of the product and use of on-screen graphics. The stream was further cross-promoted on Twitter and Instagram, uploading highlights to a combined total of nearly 21 million subscribers.
2 At TwitchCon 2018, Frito-Lay and its Doritos brand sponsored Ninja and three other streamers to participate in the Dorito Bowl, a competition in Call of Duty: Black Ops 4's Blackout mode, drawing more than 16,000 viewers.
3 PSD Underwear sponsored Ninja in 2018. PSD's "Ninja Bus" social media post achieved an engagement rate of 15.7%, and Ninja's own Instagram scored a rate of 4.4%. Ninja promoted the product using his own livestreams and social media accounts.
4 In a partnership with Red Bull, the energy drink brand, an activation featuring a special overnight Fortnite (esports games) streaming tournament hosted in Chicago drew more than 150,000 concurrent streamers.
5 UberEATS was endorsed by Ninja on a livestream in 2018, with the promotion reportedly being so successful that UberEATS ran out of codes for the promotion.

Insight #7: meaningful social justice impact is a new sponsorship category

During the early months of the pandemic, following the global attention to the death of George Floyd in Minnesota, social justice movements, particularly Black Lives Matter, a political and social movement against incidents of police brutality and racially motivated violence against black people, rose to the forefront of public attention, civic action, and passionate support from people around the globe. In sponsorship, brands invested, properties repositioned or launched, and agencies supported, in many cases starting new initiatives.

Among the many, here are a few examples, one of which two of us are deeply involved with.

- Sponsor: Nike committed $40 million to support the Black community in the United States.[2]
- Sponsor: Nestle changed the name of its "Beso de Negra" candy brand.[3]
- Property: Washington Redskins of the NFL dropped the "Redskins" name after ignoring requests to do so for many years.
- Property: Edmonton Eskimos of the CFL dropped the "Eskimos" name after ignoring requests to do so for many years.
- Agency: US-based global sport marketing agency launched "The Collective" to advance women's sport.
- Agency: our own Canada-based sponsorship agency, The T1 Agency, led by Mark Harrison, launched the Black Talent Initiative, a collaborative industry effort to increase job and internship opportunities for Black Canadians.

Insight #8: the gap between the haves and have-nots is growing

The absence of live sport has shown us something that we knew was happening, but just not by how much. Yes, the beauty of sport and the absence of those psychological moments that many of us love as fans (e.g., in the stands cheering) and participants (e.g., completing a marathon) have taught us something. The learning is that the sport industry, on the property side, is quickly becoming bimodal. Now, what do we mean by bimodal? We mean that the sport industry, from a sponsorship perspective, has always been characterized by those few properties which have high sponsor interest and the many who have to work very hard for any sponsor they can attract. Well, this gap is widening and the pandemic accelerated it. Major sport properties (major professional sport, major league tennis, golf and auto racing, the Olympic Games, etc.) continued to function and attract sponsors even without fans in venues. In fact, they were able to innovate and, in many cases, move activations from live event to digital in nature.

Most in the sport industry worldwide have been left behind. Youth sport, amateur sport clubs, local events, gyms, venues, state/provincial finals, provincial championships, school sport, learn-to-race camps, and we could go on and on. Cancelled, delayed, closed, bankrupt, reduced, virtual donations only, and so on.

Insight #9: sponsorship servicing by properties to such a level that they become essential

A slight change of gears here, an insight that draws on our collective 75+ years in the sport industry and working with, competing for, coaching, owning, volunteering for, and judging sport properties, it is clear for us that sport properties need to shift their sponsorship goals from "telling a good story" (i.e., everyone has a good story) and linking to passionate fans and/or participants (i.e., every sport property has those) to helping your sponsors solve a business problem that they have. Basically, the goal is to convince their target consumers that without their brand (i.e., your sponsor's brand), the sport event/property would not happen, and would not exist.

Insight #10: legalized sport betting is a growing sponsorship opportunity

There are different forms of sport betting including the exchange of money (e.g., casino), betting on future events (e.g., football matches), and lotteries (e.g., national lottery). One can bet with bookmaker in different ways by visiting bookmaking shops, using casino sportsbooks, calling telephone-based bookmakers, and visiting online bookmakers. However, some of the ways are legally restricted at some places. While sport betting is much more established in countries such as the UK, it is a new phenomenon in the United states. In 2018, the US Supreme Court struck down the federal law that previously banned sports betting. However, the states still make the final decision as to whether they authorize sport betting or not. As of Spring 2021, a total of 24 states authorized to host sport betting. With its emergence, sports bookmakers are investing fast in sport sponsorship.

Even as far back as 2015, few would have guessed that North America would join Europe and much of the sporting world in legalizing sport betting. But things change, and changed fast, and this is one example of that. Today, sponsorship is attracting sport betting organizations seeking awareness and association to sport properties with league sponsorships, jersey sponsorships, and naming rights. Innovative activations are starting, and we expect to see them grow rapidly in the future. The following case study provides a league sponsorship and sport betting example.

Case study 6.2[4] FanDuel, MGM Resorts, and the National Hockey League

In 2018, the NHL and FanDuel announced a multiyear partnership, making FanDuel the exclusive daily fantasy provider and official sports betting partner of the NHL. As both a daily fantasy sports and sports betting provider, FanDuel offers the NHL the potential to grow their betting offerings and drive fan engagement. FanDuel operates sports books (i.e., betting), as well as online casinos, fantasy sport leagues, and horse betting (also digital) in the United States. In recent years, FanDuel has been part of a number of mergers and acquisitions, which has brought enhanced resources to the brand and is enabling its expansion in sport betting markets in the United States.

Also, in 2018, the NHL signed a multiyear sponsorship deal with MGM Resorts, who became the NHL's official resort destination. MGM is a household name in casinos and megaresorts, with a global base of destination resorts, many of which are in Las Vegas and linked to gambling and casinos. They also have destination resorts in gambling, the gambling centers of Macau, China, and Atlantic City, USA.

These sponsorships and public commentary by the NHL support their plan to associate with sport betting to build fan engagement. For example, FanDuel, through the partnership, will be able to provide its customers with exclusive NHL content, including real-time data and VIP experiences. The sponsorship has expanded to include live streaming of out-of-market regular-season games – via FanDuel's Sportsbook platform – as part of FanDuel's efforts to become a one-stop shop for all sports and betting content.

Insight #11: invest in digital

Although intuitive by this stage, it is an insight one cannot lose sight of in sponsorship's future. The world is digital; anyone under 35 is a digital native and digital is where the future lies. This could be in the form of social media, apps, augmented reality (AR), or virtual reality (VR). Each of these is discussed in Chapter 3. Case study 6.3 from sport marketing leader Nike illustrates this.

Case study 6.3 Nike and digital[5]

Starting in March 2020, the COVID-19 pandemic forced many people around the world to stay at home. Stores shuttered. Restaurants closed. Schools moved online. Global sport apparel retailer Nike closed their stores as well to join in the effort to help curb the spread of the virus. Concurrently, Nike expanded its digital strategy, including making its Nike Training Club (NTC) app free for everyone (as opposed to its previous freemium strategy), with its published associated moto being "turn staying in into your at-home advantage" (https://www.nike.com/ca/ntc-app).

While Nike's competitors (e.g., Peloton, Lululemon) strategy focused on revenue generation through subscriptions, Nike decided to take a different approach, based on a view that the downstream benefits will exceed the subscription revenue it is forgoing by offering the app at no cost. Publicly, Nike reported that its strategy is to increase customer loyalty through delivering personalization at scale, which is built on four key pillars:

1 "Lure customers with free workouts": traditionally, Nike has had little visibility into what their customers do while wearing Nike's apparel, but the app will provide data about users' workout habits, which can lead to a personalized commerce experience. Through tracking members fitness habits, Nike will improve its ability to recommend the right products at the right time.

2 "Sign up for the workouts, stay for the sneakers": with a dedicated tab in the NTC app, customers can buy products directly through the app. Customers have begun to build a love for Nike trainers featured in the app. Now, when trainers recommend a product, customers check it out. For example, when people participate in yoga activities daily, they get connected with yoga apparel options, and then yoga products begin trending. Through this process, Nike trainers have also become legitimate influencers and personalities.

3 "Keep them coming back for more": while Nike's competitors have taken specialized approaches (e.g., yoga, running, or cycling in many cases), Nike has done the opposite, and gone broad. Every small difference Nike provides in its

workouts increases the cost of its delivery, but it also adds to the personalized experience of the consumer. Nike has also included sport-specific and skill development training, hoping to target younger audiences which may be more interested in progressing within their sport rather than general fitness.

4   "The future of the Swoosh": as Nike doubles down on its direct relationship with customers, it closed accounts with nine wholesalers in 2020. Using the NTC app, Nike is "trading physical accessibility for digital accessibility." When all is said and done, Nike has already seen a payoff: "Nike active members increased nearly 60% in [its most recent quarter], and the retailer also saw 50% of members start a workout through the training app in Q1, while recording 200% growth in demand for the retailer's commerce app."

While this case is not necessarily about sponsorship, it is an illustrative example to show how properties and sponsors can and should embrace the digital technology to enhance their business offerings.

Insight #12: sponsorship needs to be linked to the overall marketing function

Sponsorships of a brand should be integrated into the entire marketing plan of the brand. We have observed this in our experiences, but not enough. In fact, we have seen far too many situations where a sponsorship sits on its own, outside of a brand's marketing strategy and with activations that are traditional in nature. As noted in Chapter 1, sponsorship is one element of a brand's marketing communication or promotional mix. The others are advertising, sales promotion, public relations, and personal sales. Each does not work in isolation, but rather as an integral part of the bigger marketing plan. A sponsor must ensure that all forms of communications and messages are carefully linked together, whether it is communicated through sponsorship, advertising, personal sales, or any of the other approaches.

It is time to change what we observed in our experience – sponsorship put on its own. Two suggestions for brands are (i) build sponsorships as a part of your company's larger marketing plan, and (ii) when you evaluate any sponsorship, use multichannel analytics (social, digital, surveys, attendees, participants, etc.) to make sure it is resonating across all your activities.

Insight #13: differentiate servicing/fulfillment from sponsorship evaluation

This is a simple but straightforward one. Do not rely on easy-to-get data from your partners or friends such as from servicing, including your fulfillment report. Do not settle for data that will validate what you did but not critically assess whether it was a good choice or not. Do not use a set of data you get post hoc (i.e., after the sponsorship has happened). If you are asking 50,000 dollars from your sponsor, put some effort that is worth what you are asking. Do not fall for easy data. If it is easy, then less effort, which, in turn, means it is of less worth. Do sponsorship evaluation, following the seven steps discussed in Chapter 5. Case study 6.4 below provides an example of servicing/fulfillment elements, as the sponsor in this case used discounted tickets, associated advertisements during the event, and support of the Parapan American Games, via an endorsement deal with para-badminton player Pilar Jáuregui, as part of the 2019 sponsorship outlined in the case study.

Case study 6.4 LATAM Airlines and 2019 Pan American and Parapan American Games[6]

In March 2019, LATAM Airlines, an airline based in Santiago, Chile, was named the official airline of the Lima 2019 Pan American Games, joining Atos in the Gold Sponsor category. The deal was signed at a ceremony featuring a Karate demonstration by Peru's top karateka, who was also within the Top 4 World Rankings and the defending Pan Am Games Champion, as well as other Peruvian athletes. The president of Pan Am Sports, Neven Ilic, traveled to Peru's capital specifically for this signing ceremony, citing LATAM as "one of the most important airlines in the world, and we are proud that it is the Official Airline of the Games".

As the official airline of the games, LATAM transported 4,904 athletes, technical officers, and leaders of 13 countries to and from the games. This transportation included a delegation of 723 people from Mexico. LATAM Airlines was also responsible for the travel of the Pan American Torch, with its journey starting at the ruins of Teotihuacan in Mexico, before being taken to Machu Picchu via a LATAM Airlines flight.

Executives of Pan Am Sports and LATAM were quite excited about the partnership. Executive director of Lima 2019, Carlos

Neuhaus Tudela, was thankful to LATAM for their trust in the event, and logistics around athlete accommodation and travel, particularly para-athletes. The CEO of LATAM Airlines Peru, Manuel van Oordt, was excited for LATAM to be close to a large number of outstanding Latin American athletes. LATAM, with their headquarters in Lima, also felt they could not pass up the opportunity to be part of an event of this magnitude in their own backyard. LATAM Airlines can integrate their sponsorship with the other elements of promotion. For example, the airline can offer a coupon of 50% tickets discount to lucky winners from those who buy a ticket before the Games (to link with sales promotion), book a television or radio advertisement during the Games (to link with advertisement), and financially support young and up-coming athletes who will be competing in the Games (to connect to PR).

Insight #14: intellectual property is a sponsorship asset

If you are following the sport business, the public information and reporting around investments and the intellectual property value in sport is increasingly common, whether it is an investment firm with sport executives and elite athletes participating or legal decisions related to the intellectual property (IP) value of sport properties. On the investment side, public reports about special-purpose acquisition companies (SPAC) are common and include ventures including names like LeBron James, Eli Manning, and Billy Beane. On the IP side, the most discussed example is the NIL (name, image, likeness) in the NCAA, which is about athletes being able to benefit financially from their own IP. For small properties, make sure that your trademark is registered.

Insight #15: smaller sport properties can stream

Smaller sport properties do not attract mainstream media attention, rarely get daily news coverage, and do not see large number of live audiences. With the limited opportunities that they have with the mainstream media, they can invest their limited resources on social media. Particularly, followers of a social media site are those who have interest in the account that they follow. Hence, followers are users with common needs, and so are the followers of your property. Uniquely, social media allows a property to pull together the target audiences of your sport.

Streaming has opened up a new avenue for smaller sport properties to get their content out. You can stream on Facebook Live or YouTube Live. Not only is it about streaming, but you need to make sure that you have offered the opportunity as a venue that your sponsor can take advantage of. One example is the case of the Canadian Hockey League's (CHL) junior hockey league. The CHL, the leading major junior league, has 52 Canadian teams and 8 teams based in the United States. It is one of the key development pathways for professional ice hockey players. The clubs are mostly located in small cities. In early 2021, the CHL announced a new streaming partnership with Verizon as a means to get their content widely distributed.[7]

Summary of insights

The Figure 6.1 includes the 21 insights shared in the chapter. It includes the 15 insights as well as the subinsights of those with broken out ideas, for 21 total insights.

Figure 6.1 Insights on Sport Sponsorship.

As you can tell by our figure above, we are bullish on the future of sponsorship globally, but with some strong caution that we – as an industry – need to continue to "up our game" with smarter analytics, more sophisticated activations, dedicated servicing, and regular evaluation, among many more future actions.

Notes

1 https://www.upfluence.com/influencer-marketing/15-twitch-gaming-streamers-worth-watching; https://mediakix.com/blog/twitch-sponsorships-non-gaming-brands/
2 https://news.nike.com/news/nike-commitment-to-black-community
3 https://www.forbes.com/sites/elanagross/2020/06/25/nestl-will-rename-its-red-skins-chicos-and-beso-de-negra-products/?sh=61be7a1e233c
4 https://www.nhl.com/news/nhl-and-fanduel-form-multi-year-partnership/c-301623648; https://www.sportspromedia.com/news/nhl-fanduel-betting-img-arena-ice-hockey-streaming-rights#:~:text=The%20National%20Hockey%20League%20(NHL,a%20wager%20on%20an%20event;https://www.lineups.com/betting/what-the-fanduel-nhl-partnership-tells-us-about-the-direction-of-betting-in-us/
5 https://www.nike.com/ca/ntc-app; https://footwearnews.com/2020/focus/athletic-outdoor/nike-training-club-premium-app-free-1203025449/; https://marker.medium.com/how-nike-could-beat-peloton-at-its-own-game-9934b525f40
6 https://www.panamsports.org/news-sport/lima-2019-adds-two-valuable-sponsors/#:~:text=The%20Lima%202019%20Pan%20American,rights%20in%20their%20respective%20categories; https://po.travel2latam.com/nota/54149-latam-is-the-official-airline-of-the-pan-american-games-lima-2019; https://www.anocolympic.org/olympic-movement/latam-airlines-is-the-official-airline-of-the-lima-2019-pan-american-games/; https://pregames.lima2019.pe/en/news/latam-airlines-is-the-official-airline-of-the-lima-2019-pan-american-games
7 https://chl.ca/article/canadian-hockey-league-selects-verizon-media-platform-as-streaming-partner

References

Cornwell, B.T. (2021). Sponsorship marketing council of Canada presentation, March 24th, 2021.
SponsorshipX (2020). COVID impact studies. https://sponsorshipx.com/covid-19-impact-study/

Afterword
It's Game Time

Thank you for reading this book.

We hope that you gained a lot from it. Perhaps this book was your first ever introduction to the beautiful world of sports sponsorship. If you are a veteran marketer, we may have provided the insights and trending topics to ensure your knowledge base is as current as it possibly can be. The contents may help you refresh your understanding of a specific sponsorship tool, such as evaluation.

The learning and knowledge outcomes are as important to us as we assume they are to you. However, they are only a tiny part of the equation. We would say that your reading our words is only the first quarter of the journey. Like a great football team, we want to inspire you to play four full quarters.

The second quarter is an essential step. We want you to apply what you have learned here to your organization. Take these new approaches, customize one of them to first your culture, and try it out. Experiential learning is the most powerful, so experiment, execute, and evaluate. We encourage you to pull content from this book to influence your peers and superiors, or to reference our findings in discussions with your clients or sponsors. You paid for this book; you might as well use it to generate ROI.

The third quarter of any football is the most crucial. It is the vital phase of any game. Your third quarter is no less critical as this is when you build your industry network. Start with us. We want to hear from you and get to know you better. Our industry is a community, and each one of us is only as strong as our network. Now that you have had a chance to get to know us, we would love to know you. I cannot overemphasize the power of connections.

While we don't want to celebrate too early, we believe the fourth quarter is when you can put the icing on the cake. It is now the time to take what you have learned, build upon your early success in applying these lessons and utilize your growing network, pass it on to others. The sponsorship industry thrives on learning from one another and sharing best practices. You may have impostor syndrome, but you shouldn't. You will have the credentials and the experience if you tackle these first three quarters of devouring this book, applying your learnings, and building your community.

As we look back, perhaps the three of us should drop the moniker of being authors and consider ourselves to be what we are – your coaches. In that case, consider this your final pep talk before the whistle blows.

It's Game Time!

Index

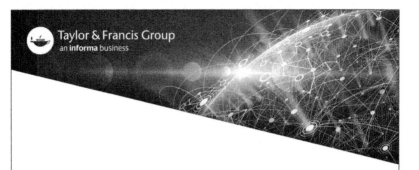